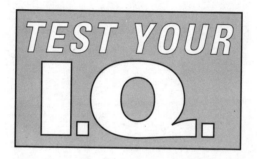

TEST YOUR I.Q.

by Alfred W. Munzert, Ph.D.

TEST YOUR I.Q.

by Alfred W. Munzert, Ph.D.

Macmillan • USA

I would like to acknowledge the invaluable contribution of Mary Colvin, whose many hours of research and professional assistance have helped to make this book possible.

Fourth Edition

Macmillan Reference USA

A Simon & Schuster Macmillan Company

1633 Broadway

New York, NY 10019-6785

An Arco Book

10   9   8   7   6   5   4   3   2   1

Library of Congress Number: 97-071466

ISBN: 0-02-861936-6

CONTENTS

INTRODUCTION

Of all the subjects that intrigue our modern society, none is more fascinating than intelligence. Specifically, what do we mean by intelligence? How is it measured? Of even greater importance—what are the implications of such measurement to the individual?

Far more than idle curiosity prompts such questions. Not only is our educational system structured to channel the intelligence of the individual into desired and productive behaviors, but the entire society tends to create a hierarchy of status and reward based upon the perceived intelligence of its members. For the individual who must cope with this complexity, the desire to know more about his or her intelligence and abilities is not just compelled by ego—it is vital knowledge that can impact every facet of existence. It is the purpose of this book not only to present an instrument for the measurement of the intelligence quotient (I.Q.) but also to offer other significant information regarding human intelligence that will be of value to the reader. If this book assists the reader to a more profound self-understanding and analysis of his or her ability to cope with the surrounding society, then it will have fulfilled its objective.

Alfred W. Munzert, Ph.D.

PART I

Self-Scoring I.Q. Test

INSTRUCTIONS

On the following pages, you will take a carefully constructed test designed to measure your intelligence. You may take this test if you are eleven years or older. Take the test only when you are in a fresh state of mind. Be sure that your testing conditions include good lighting and a quiet, comfortable work area. Please carefully observe the time restrictions and do not discuss the questions with anyone else while taking the test.

At the end of the test, you will find a complete scoring table and explanations of the answers to all of the questions. The explanations will help you understand the basis of the test. Later sections of this book will include a detailed discussion of how the test is scored and interpreted and of how I.Q. is measured. You will also find an important discussion of left-brain and right-brain functions and their relationship to intelligence scores. Although the test itself will give you a fairly accurate index of your intelligence, there are many other aspects of the human intellect—such as creativity, musical talent, and psychomotor skills—that are *not* measured by an I.Q. test. These are carefully explored in the other sections of this book. We strongly recommend that you review each of these in order to gain a complete understanding of human intelligence.

IMPORTANT!—Read These Instructions First

A. Instructions

1. You have 45 minutes to answer the 60 questions. Do *not* exceed this time limit.

2. Answer *all* questions. If you do not know the answer—guess. Guessing has been considered in the scoring. Do not leave any question unanswered.

3. If a question seems to have more than one answer or no correct answers at all, pick what you consider to be the *best* of the choices given. These questions are purposely designed to test your ability to think and reason.

B. Sample Questions

Carefully study the following sample questions before beginning the test.

I. In some questions you will be asked to make a comparison.

EXAMPLE: Which one of the five makes the best comparison?

Boat is to water as airplane is to:

SUN—GROUND—WATER—SKY—TREE

The answer is *sky*. A boat travels through water. This can be compared to an airplane that travels through the sky.

You will also be asked to compare designs.

EXAMPLE: Which one of the five makes the best comparison?

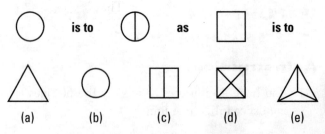

The answer is C. A circle that is divided into two parts can be compared to a square that is also divided into two parts.

II. In some questions you will be given a group of five things. Four of them will have something in common; they will be similar in some way. You will be asked to choose the one that is not similar to the other four.

EXAMPLE: Which one of the five is least like the other four?

DOG—CAR—CAT—BIRD—FISH

The answer is *car*. The others are all living creatures.

A car is not alive.

These questions may also be based on designs.

EXAMPLE: Which one of the five is least like the other four?

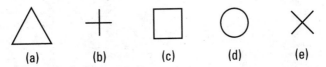

(a)   (b)   (c)   (d)   (e)

The answer is D. The others are all made with straight lines. A circle is a curved line.

III. In some questions you will be given numbers or letters which are in a certain order. They follow some pattern of arrangement. However, one of them will not fit. You will be asked to choose the one that does not fit into the pattern.

EXAMPLE: Which one of the numbers does not belong in the following series?

1—3—5—7—9—10—11—13

The answer is 10. Starting with 1, the odd numbers are arranged in order; 10 is an even number, which does not fit in the series.

IV. There will also be some problems you will be asked to solve. These will not require any difficult math. Instead, they will be testing how logical you are—that is, how well you think.

You are now ready to begin the test. Read each question carefully and write the letter of your answer or the number that you choose in the space next to the question number on the answer sheet on page 3. Tear out the answer sheet before you begin. You have 45 minutes to answer the questions.

I.Q. TEST

1. Which of the five makes the best comparison?

YYZZZYZZY is to 221112112 as YYZZYZZY is to:

221221122   **22112122**   **22112112**   **112212211**   **212211212**

(a)   (b)   (c)   (d)   (e)

---

2. Which of the five is least like the other four?

NICKEL   **TIN**   **STEEL**   **IRON**   **COPPER**

(a)   (b)   (c)   (d)   (e)

---

3. Which of the five designs makes the best comparison?

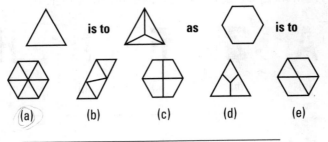

(a)   (b)   (c)   (d)   (e)

---

4. Which of the five designs is least like the other four?

N   A   V   H   F

(a)   (b)   (c)   (d)   (e)

5. Jerry received both the 15th highest and the 15th lowest mark in the class. How many students are in the class?

15	25	29	30	32
(a)	(b)	(c)	(d)	(e)

---

6. Which of the five is least like the other four?

DICTIONARY	BIOGRAPHY	ATLAS	ALMANAC	DIRECTORY
(a)	(b)	(c)	(d)	(e)

---

7. Which of the five is least like the other four?

A	Z	F	N	H
(a)	(b)	(c)	(d)	(e)

---

8. Which of the five makes the best comparison?

Foot is to hand as leg is to:

ELBOW	PIANO	TOE	FINGER	ARM
(a)	(b)	(c)	(d)	(e)

9. Which of the five designs makes the best comparison?

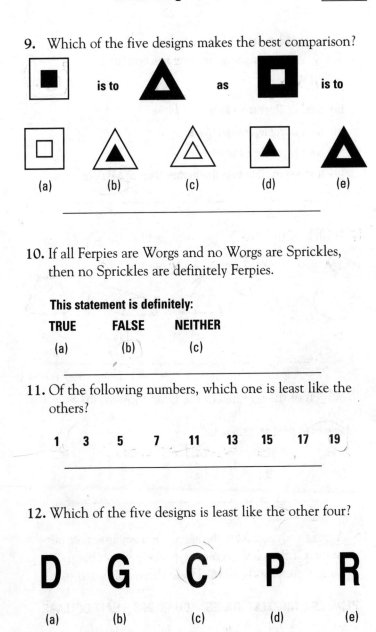

10. If all Ferpies are Worgs and no Worgs are Sprickles, then no Sprickles are definitely Ferpies.

This statement is definitely:

TRUE   FALSE   NEITHER

(a)   (b)   (c)

11. Of the following numbers, which one is least like the others?

1   3   5   7   11   13   15   17   19

12. Which of the five designs is least like the other four?

D   **G**   **C**   **P**   **R**

(a)   (b)   (c)   (d)   (e)

13. Terry is older than Mark and Sam is younger than Terry. Which of the following statements is most accurate?

    (a) **Sam is older than Mark.**
    (b) **Sam is younger than Mark.**
    (c) **Sam is as old as Mark.**
    (d) **It is impossible to tell whether Sam or Mark is older.**

14. Which of the five designs is least like the other four?

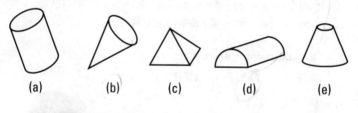

(a)   (b)   (c)   (d)   (e)

15. Which of the five makes the best comparison?

    Leap is to peal as 8326 is to:

2368	6283	2683	6328	3628
(a)	(b)	(c)	(d)	(e)

16. Anne received $0.59 change from a supermarket purchase. Of the eleven coins she received in change, three were exactly alike. These three coins had to be:

PENNIES	NICKELS	DIMES	QUARTERS	HALF DOLLARS
(a)	(b)	(c)	(d)	(e)

17. Which of the five is least like the other four?

PECK	OUNCE	PINT	CUP	QUART
(a)	(b)	(c)	(d)	(e)

18. Three enemy messages were intercepted at communications headquarters. The code was broken, and it was found that "Berok tenlis krux" means "Secret attack Wednesday" and "Baroom zax tenlis" means "Secret plans included" and "Gradnor berok plil elan" means "Wednesday victory is ours." What does "krux" mean?

SECRET	WEDNESDAY	NOTHING	ATTACK	PLANS
(a)	(b)	(c)	(d)	(e)

19. Which of the five makes the best comparison?

Love is to hate as valor is to:

COURAGE	SECURITY	COWARDICE	ANGER	TERROR
(a)	(b)	(c)	(d)	(e)

20. The price of an article was cut 50% for a sale. By what percent must the item be increased to again sell at the original price?

25%	50%	75%	100%	200%
(a)	(b)	(c)	(d)	(e)

21. Which of the five designs makes the best comparison?

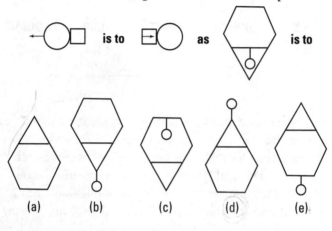

(a)   (b)   (c)   (d)   (e)

---

22. Which of the five is least like the other four?

SQUASH	PUMPKIN	TOMATO	CUCUMBER	CORN
(a)	(b)	(c)	(d)	(e)

---

23. Which of the five makes the best comparison?

Hole is to donut as pages are to:

STORY	WORDS	CONTENTS	INDEX	COVER
(a)	(b)	(c)	(d)	(e)

---

24. Kim was sent to the store to get 11 large cans of fruit. Kim could carry only 2 cans at a time. How many trips to the store did Kim have to make?

5	5½	6	6½	7
(a)	(b)	(c)	(d)	(e)

25. Which of the five designs makes the best comparison?

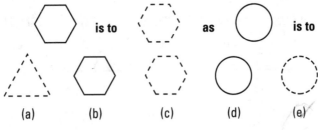

26. If all Pleeps are Floops and all Floops are Leepies, then all Pleeps are definitely Leepies.

This statement is definitely:

TRUE	FALSE	NEITHER
(a)	(b)	(c)

27. Which of the five designs is least like the other four?

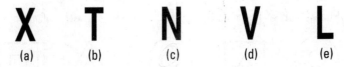

28. Jim, John, Jerry, and Joe together bought a basket of 144 apples. Jim received 10 more apples than John, 26 more than Jerry, and 32 more than Joe. How many apples did Jim receive?

73	63	53	43	27
(a)	(b)	(c)	(d)	(e)

29. Which of the five is least like the other four?

TOUCH	SEE	HEAR	EAT	SMELL
(a)	(b)	(c)	(d)	(e)

30. Which of the five makes the best comparison?

Daughter is to father as niece is to:

NEPHEW	COUSIN	UNCLE	MOTHER	BROTHER
(a)	(b)	(c)	(d)	(e)

31. Which of the five designs is least like the other four?

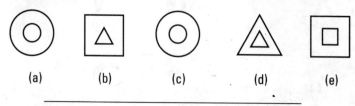

| (a) | (b) | (c) | (d) | (e) |

32. Which number does not belong in the following series?

4　　5　　8　　10　　11　　16　　19　　32　　36

33. Which of the five makes the best comparison?

Bark is to tree as scales are to:

GILLS	ELEPHANT	BUTCHER	FISH	SKIN
(a)	(b)	(c)	(d)	(e)

---

34. Which if the five is least like the other four?

TURKEY	DUCK	CHICKEN	PHEASANT	GOOSE
(a)	(b)	(c)	(d)	(e)

---

35. The secher vlooped quaply berak the kriggly lool. Then the secher _____ flaxly down the kleek.

Which word belongs in the space?

VLOOPED	QUAPLY	BERAK	LOOL	KRIGGLY
(a)	(b)	(c)	(d)	(e)

---

36. The fish has a head 9 inches long. The tail is equal to the size of the head plus one-half the size of the body. The body is the size of the head plus the tail. How long is the fish?

27 inches	54 inches	63 inches	72 inches	81 inches
(a)	(b)	(c)	(d)	(e)

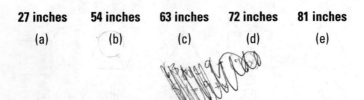

37. Which of the five designs is least like the other four?

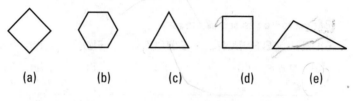

   (a)   (b)   (c)   (d)   (e)

38. If you rearrange the letters in "NAICH," you would have the name of a(n):

COUNTRY	OCEAN	STATE	CITY	ANIMAL
(a)	(b)	(c)	(d)	(e)

39. Jack is 15 years old, three times as old as his sister. How old will Jack be when he is twice as old as his sister?

18	20	24	26	30
(a)	(b)	(c)	(d)	(e)

40. Which of the five designs makes the best comparison?

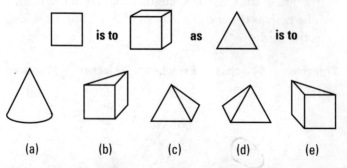

   (a)   (b)   (c)   (d)   (e)

41. Slok are more zitful than mulk, but pringling flex are most _____ of all.

Which word belongs in the blank space?

SLOK	ZITFUL	MULK	PRINGLING	FLEX
(a)	(b)	(c)	(d)	(e)

---

42. Which of the five makes the best comparison?

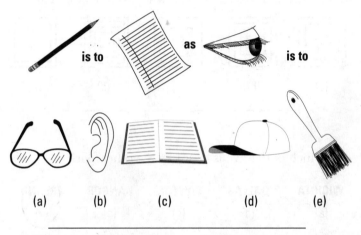

(a)	(b)	(c)	(d)	(e)

---

43. If you rearrange the letters in "SHORE," you would have the name of a(n):

COUNTRY	OCEAN	STATE	CITY	ANIMAL
(a)	(b)	(c)	(d)	(e)

---

44. Which number does not belong in the following series?

1   3   5   7   9   11   12   13   15

45. Which of the five makes the best comparison?

Gas is to car as food is to:

MOUTH	STOMACH	ENERGY	BODY	TEETH
(a)	(b)	(c)	(d)	(e)

_____

46. Which of the five designs is least like the other four?

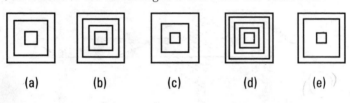

(a)	(b)	(c)	(d)	(e)

_____

47. Which of the five is least like the other four?

WICHITA	DALLAS	CANTON	BANGOR	FRESNO
(a)	(b)	(c)	(d)	(e)

_____

48. If some Tripples are Tropples and all Bolars are Tropples, then some Tripples are definitely Bolars.

This statement is:

TRUE	FALSE	NEITHER
(a)	(c)	(c)

49. Which of the five designs makes the best comparison?

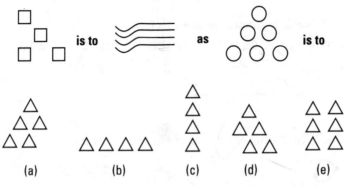

(a) (b) (c) (d) (e)

---

50. Which of the five makes the best comparison?

Sack is to sad as turn is to:

TACK	UP	TURF	BURN	TOY
(a)	(b)	(c)	(d)	(e)

---

51. Which of the five designs is least like the other four?

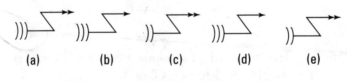

(a) (b) (c) (d) (e)

---

52. Which letter does not belong in the following series?

B   E   H   K   M   N   Q   T

53. Which of the five makes the best comparison?

Pillow is to pillowcase as arm is to:

BODY	SLEEVE	HAND	GLOVE	RING
(a)	(b)	(c)	(d)	(e)

---

54. Which of the five is least like the other four?

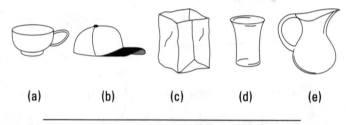

(a)	(b)	(c)	(d)	(e)

---

55. Which of the five is least like the other four?

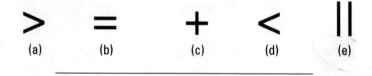

(a)	(b)	(c)	(d)	(e)

---

56. If all Truples are Glogs and some Glogs are Glips, then some Truples are definitely Glips.

This statement is:

TRUE	FALSE	NEITHER
(a)	(b)	(c)

57. If you rearrange the letters in "TALCATIN," you would have the name of a:

COUNTRY	OCEAN	STATE	CITY	ANIMAL
(a)	(b)	(c)	(d)	(e)

---

58. Which of the five is least like the other four?

ARTIST	GOLFER	NEWSCASTER	DANCER	MECHANIC
(a)	(b)	(c)	(d)	(e)

---

59. Which of the five does not belong in the series?

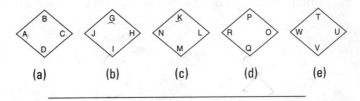

(a)	(b)	(c)	(d)	(e)

---

60. Which of the five is least like the other four?

WATER	SUN	GASOLINE	WIND	CEMENT
(a)	(b)	(c)	(d)	(e)

ANSWERS AND EXPLANATIONS

1. Which of the five makes the best comparison?

YYZZZYZZY is to 221112112 as YYZZYZZY is to:

221221122	22112122	22112112	112212211	212211212
(a)	(b)	(c)	(d)	(e)

Answer: **C** *Substitute numbers for letters: Y = 2; Z = 1.*

---

2. Which of the five is least like the other four?

NICKEL	**TIN**	**STEEL**	**IRON**	**COPPER**
(a)	(b)	(c)	(d)	(e)

Answer: **C** *(Steel) The others are simple metals; steel is an alloy (combination of two metals).*

---

3. Which of the five designs makes the best comparison?

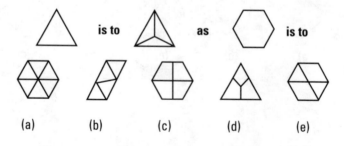

(a)   (b)   (c)   (d)   (e)

Answer: **A** *The six-sided hexagon is divided into six equal parts by lines drawn from its outside vertices, just as the three-sided triangle is divided into three equal parts by lines drawn from its outside vertices.*

---

4. Which of the five designs is least like the other four?

N   A   V   H   F

  (a)   (b)   (c)   (d)   (e)

Answer: ***C***   *All the others are made with three lines; V is made with two lines.*

5. Jerry received both the 15th highest and the 15th lowest mark in the class. How many students are in the class?

15	25	29	30	32
(a)	(b)	(c)	(d)	(e)

Answer: ***C***   *There are 14 students higher and 14 students lower. Jerry is the 29th student; the one in the middle.*

6. Which of the five is least like the other four?

DICTIONARY	BIOGRAPHY	ATLAS	ALMANAC	DIRECTORY
(a)	(b)	(c)	(d)	(e)

Answer: ***B***   *All the others are reference books. A biography is a narrative.*

7. Which of the five is least like the other four?

A   Z   F   N   H

  (a)   (b)   (c)   (d)   (e)

Answer: ***A***   *The others are consonants; A is a vowel.*

8. Which of the five makes the best comparison?

Foot is to hand as leg is to:

ELBOW	**PIANO**	**TOE**	**FINGER**	**ARM**
(a)	(b)	(c)	(d)	(e)

Answer: ***E***   *A foot is attached to a leg; a hand is attached to an arm.*

9. Which of the five designs makes the best comparison?

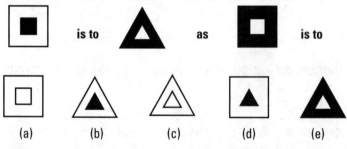

  (a)   (b)   (c)   (d)   (e)

Answer: ***B***   *The square changes to a triangle and the shading is reversed.*

10. If all Ferpies are Worgs and no Worgs are Sprickles, then no Sprickles are definitely Ferpies.

This statement is definitely:

TRUE	FALSE	NEITHER
(a)	(b)	(c)

Answer: *A* *Example: If all dogs are animals and no animals are plants, then no plants are definitely dogs.*

11. Of the following numbers, which one is least like the others?

1   3   5   7   11   13   15   17   19

Answer: *15* *The others are prime numbers—they can be divided only by themselves and 1. Fifteen is not a prime number. It can be divided by itself, 1, 3, and 5.*

12. Which of the five designs is least like the other four?

D   **G**   **C**   **P**   **R**

(a)   (b)   (c)   (d)   (e)

Answer: *C* *The others are all made from a straight line and a curve. C is only a curve.*

13. Terry is older than Mark and Sam is younger than Terry. Which of the following statements is most accurate?

   (a) Sam is older than Mark.

   (b) Sam is younger than Mark.

   (c) Sam is as old as Mark.

   (d) It is impossible to tell whether Sam or Mark is older.

Answer: **D**   *Without more information it is impossible to tell. We only know that both Mark and Sam are younger than Terry.*

---

14. Which of the five designs is least like the other four?

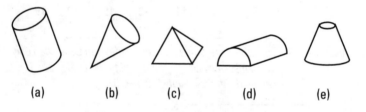

   (a)   (b)   (c)   (d)   (e)

Answer: **C**   *It is made with only straight lines. The others are made with straight lines and curves.*

---

15. Which of the five makes the best comparison?

   Leap is to peal as 8326 is to:

2368	6283	2683	6328	3628
(a)	(b)	(c)	(d)	(e)

Answer: **D**   *Substitute numbers for letters: L = 8, E = 3, A = 2, P = 6. Peal = 6328.*

---

16. Anne received $0.59 change from a supermarket purchase. Of the eleven coins she received in change, three were exactly alike. These three coins had to be:

PENNIES	NICKELS	DIMES	QUARTERS	HALF DOLLARS
(a)	(b)	(c)	(d)	(e)

Answer: **B**   Four dimes, three nickels, and four pennies is the only solution.

17. Which of the five is least like the other four?

PECK	OUNCE	PINT	CUP	QUART
(a)	(b)	(c)	(d)	(e)

Answer: **A**   Peck is the only dry measure; the others measure both liquid and dry quantities.

18. Three enemy messages were intercepted at communications headquarters. The code was broken, and it was found that "Berok tenlis krux" means "Secret attack Wednesday" and "Baroom zax tenlis" means "Secret plans included" and "Gradnor berok plil elan" means "Wednesday victory is ours." What does "krux" mean?

SECRET	WEDNESDAY	NOTHING	ATTACK	PLANS
(a)	(b)	(c)	(d)	(e)

Answer: **D**   tenlis = secret; berok = Wednesday; krux = attack

19. Which of the five makes the best comparison?

Love is to hate as valor is to:

COURAGE	SECURITY	COWARDICE	ANGER	TERROR
(a)	(b)	(c)	(d)	(e)

Answer: **C**   *Love is the opposite of hate. Valor is the opposite of cowardice.*

20. The price of an article was cut 50% for a sale. By what percent must the item be increased to again sell at the original price?

25%	50%	75%	100%	200%
(a)	(b)	(c)	(d)	(e)

Answer: **D**   *Example: A $20.00 item cut 50% will sell for $10.00. To again sell for $20.00, the item must be increased by $10.00, which is 100% of $10.00.*

21. Which of the five designs makes the best comparison?

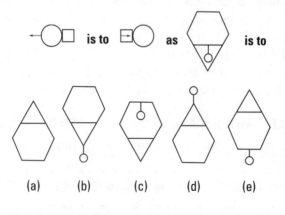

| (a) | (b) | (c) | (d) | (e) |

Answer: **E** *The position of the geometric figures is reversed. The line figuration remains on the same side of the configuration, but is reversed.*

---

22. Which of the five is least like the other four?

SQUASH	PUMPKIN	TOMATO	CUCUMBER	CORN
(a)	(b)	(c)	(d)	(e)

Answer: **E** *Corn. The others grow on vines. Corn grows on a stalk.*

---

23. Which of the five makes the best comparison?

Hole is to donut as pages are to:

STORY	WORDS	CONTENTS	INDEX	COVER
(a)	(b)	(c)	(d)	(e)

Answer: **E** *The hole is inside the doughnut, and the pages are inside the cover.*

---

24. Kim was sent to the store to get 11 large cans of fruit. Kim could carry only 2 cans at a time. How many trips to the store did Kim have to make?

5	5½	6	6½	7
(a)	(b)	(c)	(d)	(e)

Answer: **C** *$11 \div 2 = 5\frac{1}{2}$. It takes 6 trips; a half trip won't get the last can home.*

---

25. Which of the five designs makes the best comparison?

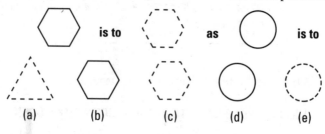

| (a) | (b) | (c) | (d) | (e) |

Answer: **E**   *It is a comparison of the same figure, solid to broken line.*

26. If all Pleeps are Floops and all Floops are Leepies, then all Pleeps are definitely Leepies.

This statement is definitely:

TRUE	**FALSE**	**NEITHER**
(a)	(b)	(c)

Answer: **A**   *Example: "If all dogs are mammals and all mammals are animals, then all dogs are definitely animals."*

27. Which of the five designs is least like the other four?

X   T   N   V   L

| (a) | (b) | (c) | (d) | (e) |

Answer: **C**   *All the others are made with two lines; N is made with three lines.*

28. Jim, John, Jerry, and Joe together bought a basket of 144 apples. Jim received 10 more apples than John, 26 more than Jerry, and 32 more than Joe. How many apples did Jim receive?

73	**63**	**53**	**43**	**27**
(a)	(b)	(c)	(d)	(e)

Answer: **C** *Jim received 53; John received 53 – 10 or 43; Jerry received 53 – 26 or 27; Joe received 53 – 32 or 21. 53 + 43 + 27 + 21 = 144. This problem may be solved algebraically as well.*

29. Which of the five is least like the other four?

TOUCH	**SEE**	**HEAR**	**EAT**	**SMELL**
(a)	(b)	(c)	(d)	(e)

Answer: **D** *The others are senses; eating is a body function.*

30. Which of the five makes the best comparison?

Daughter is to father as niece is to:

NEPHEW	**COUSIN**	**UNCLE**	**MOTHER**	**BROTHER**
(a)	(b)	(c)	(d)	(e)

Answer: **C** *Daughter is the female child of father; niece is the female child of uncle.*

31. Which of the five designs is least like the other four?

(a)   (b)   (c)   (d)   (e)

Answer: **B**   *The small figure inside the other figures is the same as the large figure it is inside.*

---

32. Which number does not belong in the following series?

4   5   8   10   11   16   19   32   36

Answer: **11**   *The order is plus one, double the first figure; plus two, double the third figure; plus three, double the fifth figure; plus four.*

---

33. Which of the five makes the best comparison?

Bark is to tree as scales are to:

GILLS   ELEPHANT   BUTCHER   FISH   SKIN
(a)   (b)   (c)   (d)   (e)

Answer: **D**   *Bark is on the outside of a tree; scales are on the outside of a fish.*

34. Which if the five is least like the other four?

TURKEY	DUCK	CHICKEN	PHEASANT	GOOSE
(a)	(b)	(c)	(d)	(e)

Answer: **D** *The others are or can be domesticated; pheasant is wild.*

35. The secher vlooped quaply berak the kriggly lool. Then the secher _____ flaxly down the kleek.

Which word belongs in the space?

VLOOPED	QUAPLY	BERAK	LOOL	KRIGGLY
(a)	(b)	(c)	(d)	(e)

Answer: **A** *A verb must go in the space. Example: The teacher walked quickly toward the open door. Then the teacher walked quickly down the hall.*

36. The fish has a head 9 inches long. The tail is equal to the size of the head plus one-half the size of the body. The body is the size of the head plus the tail. How long is the fish?

27 inches	54 inches	63 inches	72 inches	81 inches
(a)	(b)	(c)	(d)	(e)

Answer: **D** *The head is 9 inches. The tail is 18 inches + 9 inches = 27 inches. The body is 9 inches + 19 inches + 9 inches = 36 inches. 9 inches + 27 inches + 36 inches = 72 inches. This may be solved algebraically as well.*

37. Which of the five designs is least like the other four?

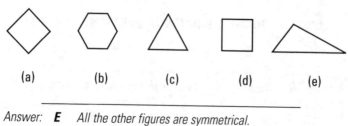

(a)   (b)   (c)   (d)   (e)

Answer: **E**   *All the other figures are symmetrical.*

---

38. If you rearrange the letters in "NAICH," you would have the name of a(n):

COUNTRY	OCEAN	STATE	CITY	ANIMAL
(a)	(b)	(c)	(d)	(e)

Answer: **A**   *"NAICH" = "CHINA."*

---

39. Jack is 15 years old, three times as old as his sister. How old will Jack be when he is twice as old as his sister?

18	20	24	26	30
(a)	(b)	(c)	(d)	(e)

Answer: **B**   *Jack is ten years older than his sister. In five years Jack will be 20, and his sister who is now 5 will be 10.*

---

40. Which of the five designs makes the best comparison?

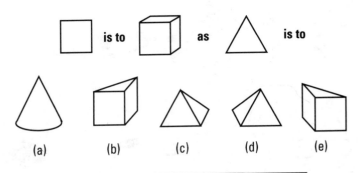

□   is to   (cube)   as   △   is to

| (a) | (b) | (c) | (d) | (e) |

Answer: **C**   *The square is a direct frontal view of the cube that is then seen from the right. The triangle is a direct frontal view of the pyramid then seen from the right.*

41. Slok are more zitful than mulk, but pringling flex are most _____ of all.

Which word belongs in the blank space?

SLOK	ZITFUL	MULK	PRINGLING	FLEX
(a)	(b)	(c)	(d)	(e)

Answer: **B**   *An adverb is required. Example: Nickels are more valuable than pennies, but twenty dollars are most valuable of all.*

42. Which of the five makes the best comparison?

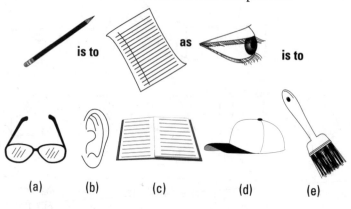

(a) (b) (c) (d) (e)

Answer: **C** *A person uses a pencil for the purpose of writing; a person uses an eye for the purpose of reading.*

43. If you rearrange the letters in "SHORE," you would have the name of a(n):

COUNTRY	OCEAN	STATE	CITY	ANIMAL
(a)	(b)	(c)	(d)	(e)

Answer: **E** *"SHORE" = "HORSE."*

44. Which number does not belong in the following series?

1   3   5   7   9   11   12   13   15

Answer: **12** *The series is made from counting by twos.*

45. Which of the five makes the best comparison?

Gas is to car as food is to:

MOUTH	**STOMACH**	**ENERGY**	**BODY**	**TEETH**
(a)	(b)	(c)	(d)	(e)

Answer: **D**   *Gas provides energy for a car; food provides energy for a body.*

46. Which of the five designs is least like the other four?

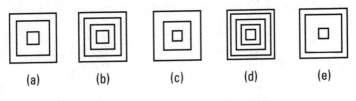

(a)	(b)	(c)	(d)	(e)

Answer: **B**   *All the others have an odd number of squares; B has an even number.*

47. Which of the five is least like the other four?

WICHITA	**DALLAS**	**CANTON**	**BANGOR**	**FRESNO**
(a)	(b)	(c)	(d)	(e)

Answer: **A**   *All the others have six letters; Wichita has seven.*

48. If some Tripples are Tropples and all Bolars are Tropples, then some Tripples are definitely Bolars.

This statement is:

TRUE	FALSE	NEITHER
(a)	(b)	(c)

Answer: **B** *Example: "If some cars are green and all leaves are green, then some cars are definitely leaves."*

---

49. Which of the five designs makes the best comparison?

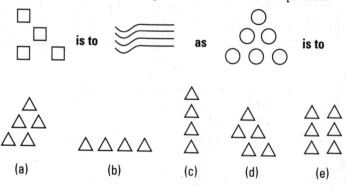

(a)	(b)	(c)	(d)	(e)

Answer: **E** *Four figures change into four figures. Six figures change into six figures.*

---

50. Which of the five makes the best comparison?

Sack is to sad as turn is to:

TACK	UP	TURF	BURN	TOY
(a)	(b)	(c)	(d)	(e)

Answer: **B**   Sad *can be combined with* sack *to make the word "sad-sack." Up* can be combined with turn *to make the word "upturn."*

---

51. Which of the five designs is least like the other four?

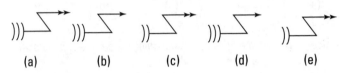

(a)   (b)   (c)   (d)   (e)

Answer: **A**   *It does not have a twin.*

---

52. Which letter does not belong in the following series?

B   E   H   K   M   N   Q   T

Answer: **M**   *The series is made up of every fourth letter of the alphabet starting with B.*

---

53. Which of the five makes the best comparison?

Pillow is to pillowcase as arm is to:

BODY   **SLEEVE**   **HAND**   **GLOVE**   **RING**

(a)   (b)   (c)   (d)   (e)

Answer: **B**   *A pillow fits inside a pillowcase. An arm fits inside a sleeve.*

54. Which of the five is least like the other four?

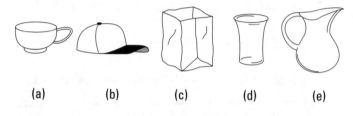

(a)	(b)	(c)	(d)	(e)

Answer: **B**   *All the others hold something inside. The cap fits on top of a head.*

55. Which of the five is least like the other four?

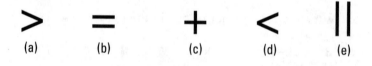

(a)	(b)	(c)	(d)	(e)

Answer: **C**   *The others all show mathematical relationships. + is a mathematical operation.*

56. If all Truples are Glogs and some Glogs are Glips, then some Truples are definitely Glips.

This statement is:

TRUE	FALSE	NEITHER
(a)	(b)	(c)

Answer: **B**   *Example: "If all cats are animals and some animals are dogs, then some cats are definitely dogs."*

57. If you rearrange the letters in "TALCATIN," you would have the name of a:

COUNTRY   **OCEAN**   **STATE**   **CITY**   **ANIMAL**
(a)   (b)   (c)   (d)   (e)

Answer: **B**   _"TALCATIN" = "ATLANTIC."_

58. Which of the five is least like the other four?

ARTIST   **GOLFER**   **NEWSCASTER**   **DANCER**   **MECHANIC**
(a)   (b)   (c)   (d)   (e)

Answer: **C**   _All the others must use their hands and/or body but not words to perform their jobs. The newscaster must use words._

59. Which of the five does not belong in the series?

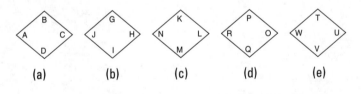

(a)   (b)   (c)   (d)   (e)

Answer: **D**   _The others have a sequence of letters in alphabetical order starting at the top and going clockwise._

60. Which of the five is least like the other four?

WATER   **SUN**   **GASOLINE**   **WIND**   **CEMENT**
(a)   (b)   (c)   (d)   (e)

Answer: **E**   _The others can all be used as sources of energy._

SCORING INSTRUCTIONS

Count up the number of questions that you answered correctly. Find that number in the column appropriate to your age and circle the number. Then, directly to the right in the I.Q. column, you will locate your correct I.Q. rating. For example, if you are 14 years old and had 32 answers correct, you locate 32 in the 14-year-old column and find that you have an I.Q. rating of 114.

AGE						I.Q.
11	**12**	**13**	**14**	**15**	**16+ Adult**	
8	10	13	15	17	19	80
9	11	14	16	18	20	82
10	12	15	17	19	21	84
11	13	16	18	20	22	86
12	14	17	19	21	23	88
13	15	18	20	22	24	90
14	16	19	21	23	25	92
15	17	20	22	24	26	94
16	18	21	23	25	27	96
17	19	22	24	26	28	98
18	20	23	25	27	29	100
19	21	24	26	28	30	102
20	22	25	27	29	31	104
21	23	26	28	30	32	106
22	24	27	29	31	33	108
23	25	28	30	32	34	110

Part I

AGE						I.Q.
11	12	13	14	15	16+ Adult	
24	26	29	31	33	35	112
25	27	30	32	34	36	114
26	28	31	33	35	37	116
27	29	32	34	36	38	118
28	30	33	35	37	39	120
29	31	34	36	38	40	122
30	32	35	37	39	41	124
31	33	36	38	40	42	126
32	34	37	39	41	43	128
33	35	38	40	42	44	130
34	36	39	41	43	45	132
35	37	40	42	44	46	134
36	38	41	43	45	47	136
37	39	42	44	46	48	138
38	40	43	45	47	49	140
39	41	44	46	48	50	142
40	42	45	47	49	51	144
41	43	46	48	50	52	146
42	44	47	49	51	53	148
43	45	48	50	52	54	150
44	46	49	51	53	55	154
45	47	50	52	54	56	158
46	48	51	53	55	57	160
47	49	52	54	56	58+	165+

PART II

Intelligence: Its Measurement and Meaning

MEASURING INTELLIGENCE

The measurement of intelligence has traditionally been put into the same category as top-secret, classified government information. I.Q. scores have been cloaked in a mystery of psychological terminology and ownership, and the general public has been left in awe of the idea and in ignorance of the results of individual testing. A certain amount of professional discretion is justified, as the results obtained from one test or from a set of individual intelligence tests need to be evaluated and interpreted within a context of many other facets of individual and group behavior.

In the more enlightened climate of recent times, people have the right to know their own I.Q. test scores as well as those of their children. It would be a serious breach of professional responsibility, however, to indiscriminately disclose these scores either to parents or to children. Children are generally unequipped with the necessary knowledge, maturity, and experience to be able to understand or to respond to the meaning of I.Q. scores. Parents, while entitled to know, are also entitled to a full explanation of what their children's I.Q. scores mean within the context of the learning environment, behavior, and achievement.

A knowledge of one's I.Q. has many advantages. Within the process of human development, an understanding of one's own potential and one's own limitations can be of enormous personal value. We all have both upward potential and personal limitations; I.Q. is but one of many indicators of both of these. It is important to know and to understand that many other factors come into play and are important to success and happiness. Motivation, sensitivity, industriousness, and capacity for love are among those factors and are among the abilities not measured by standard intelligence tests.

Intelligence *per se* is important only if used and applied to the life tasks that confront an individual each day.

There is no real mystery to the measurement of intelligence. Essentially, any test with a large number of questions and problems that requires a person to use different intellectual skills to arrive at answers can be used to generate a test of intelligence. A test that provides questions that tap areas of perception, spatial awareness, language ability, numerical ability, and memory and that requires a person to use comparisons, sequencing, classification, computation, problem-solving methods, comprehension, association, completion, reasoning, logic, analogy, evaluation, judgment, etc., in various content areas can be refined into a test of intelligence.

The test you just took is a paper-and-pencil test typical of those given either to a single individual or to a group of persons at the same sitting. In addition to paper-and-pencil tests that use the preceding kinds of materials for questions, there are also individual I.Q. tests, given on a one-to-one basis, that include "performance" kinds of problem situations. Individual tests allow for the testing of nonreaders or for testing people who have difficulty with reading or with the language. Individual tests may test auditory and retentive skills by requiring the person being tested to listen to a sequence of numbers and then to repeat that sequence. Other performance items may include puzzle completion and block structure replication. These tend to test abilities not measured by paper-and-pencil tests, such as the motor skills that relate to mechanics and to the fine arts media. People who solve problems through pictures, objects, and emotions rather than by using numerical and language concepts are candidates for individual testing. These people often have a high degree of intelligence that cannot be measured with the more economical, traditional language-oriented paper-and-pencil type of test.

Intelligence tests do not measure creativity, although certain creative skills may be brought into play in order to successfully solve specific problems. The nature of creativity and its relationship to intelligence will be discussed later.

If you had picked up a book on intelligence published 25 or more years ago, the chances are that creativity would not have been discussed, at least not in any great detail. This is because creativity was associated with high performance in the visual and performing arts and was not considered an integral part of the behaviors associated with intelligence. However, research conducted since the late 1950s, along with observations based upon experience, has shed new light upon the nature of creativity and its relationship to performance in all areas of human endeavor. In the next section, we shall explore the entire range of intelligence in order to give you a fuller understanding of its meaning and its measurement.

YOUR INTELLIGENCE SCORE (I.Q.)

Now that you have taken the intelligence test at the beginning of this book, you must be curious to know the meaning of your score or I.Q. Rest assured, you are indeed intelligent. Two indicators of intelligent behavior are *curiosity* and *language* or *reading ability*. Without these two qualities, you would not even be reading this book. Where you stand in relation to other people can be explained quite simply. The following graph shows how intelligence is distributed among the general population.

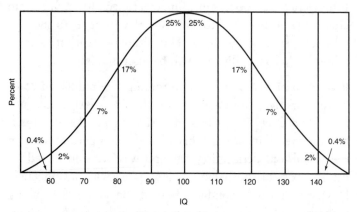

Distribution of Intelligence in the General Population

The graph shows what is called a classical bell-shaped curve. It is based on laws of probability that test out in actual life. Most people have test scores or I.Q.s that fall into the middle of the curve. This means that average intelligence is found in approximately 50% of the population and ranges between an I.Q. of 90 and 110, with a score of 100 being the "magic" number of average intelligence.

The test score, or I.Q., stands for Intelligence Quotient. It is a specific numerical measurement of a less-than-specific concept—intelligence. Although I.Q. is an indicator of innate ability and potential, it is not a pure measure. Even the best test of innate ability is contaminated by specific ability factors and by information and skills gained through experience and learning. Nonetheless, I.Q. is a reasonably good descriptive and predictive measure. I.Q. is computed by the following mathematical formula:

$$\text{I.Q.} = \frac{\text{mental age}}{\text{chronological age}} \times 100$$

Chronological age, of course, is actual age in years. Mental age is a construct based on test responses. Test questions are scientifically analyzed and determinations are made as to which problems a person of a certain age can be expected to answer successfully. After considerable statistical analysis, tests are "normed" or "standardized." This is done by administering questions designated at a certain age level to many individuals of that age. For example, how many correct answers do 10-year-olds give to items considered to be problems that an average 10-year-old should be able to successfully complete? If a 10-year-old takes the test and correctly completes the items a 10-year-old should be able to do, but no more, that indicates a mental age of 10. The formula is worked as follows:

$$\text{I.Q.} = \frac{10}{10} \text{ (or 1)} \times 100$$

$$\text{I.Q.} = 100$$

If, however, a 10-year-old takes the test and completes not only the items that a 10-year-old should be able to do but also all the items that a 13-year-old should be able to do, that individual has a mental age of 13, and the formula is worked as follows:

$$\text{I.Q.} = \frac{13}{10} \text{ (or 1.3)} \times 100$$

$$\text{I.Q.} = 130$$

If a 10-year-old takes the test but can complete only the items that an average 8-year-old should be able to do, the mental age is 8, and the formula is worked as follows:

$$\text{I.Q.} = \frac{8}{10} \text{ (or 0.8)} \times 100$$

$$\text{I.Q.} = 80$$

As was already stated, the average I.Q. is between 90 and 110. A score between 110 and 119 indicates bright intelligence. A score between 120 and 129 indicates superior intelligence. A score of 130 or over is indicative of giftedness. However, some tests vary slightly, and intellectual giftedness might be shown in a score of 135 and above, or 140 and above.

Those persons who score over 160 are endowed with superior giftedness, often described as being in the "genius" category. However, the critical factor of intelligence is its development and use. Without development, application, and productivity, high intelligence is a valueless characteristic, both to the individual and to society.

An individual who scores between 80 and 89 is usually considered a slow learner. Scores under 80 indicate varying degrees of mental handicap. However, these interpretations are made in relation to the person's *exhibited* abilities as measured on the test and their relationship to the abilities necessary for successful learning in a regular school situation. There are many reasons why I.Q., particularly the results of *one* test, may not indicate a true level of intelligence and potential capability. For this reason, one I.Q. test score should never be used to label and place an individual in a permanent school or life setting. Even a pattern of scores should be evaluated against such other factors as behavior, interest, thinking style, and actual production.

For I.Q. scores to be most meaningful and helpful to those working with the individuals involved, it is best that a pattern of test scores be established over a period of time. This is one reason why it is important for youngsters to be present each time the test is administered in school. There are many reasons why the pattern of scores is important.

Scores will normally vary somewhat on different occasions and among different tests. There should, however, be an exhibited range of scores within about a 20-point variation. Reasons for this normal range of variation result from the following facts:

1. There are some differences in the tests themselves.

2. Differences in testing conditions will influence an individual's performance on tests at different times.

3. Tests that are given to groups may be less accurate than tests that are individually given.

4. The physical and mental well-being of the person taking the test will vary from one time to another.

A variation of more than 20 points is often an indication that more careful observation and/or testing needs to be conducted. For example, an extreme downward variation in test scores may indicate possible physical and/or psychological problems that require further investigation. An extreme upward variation suggests an upper limit of abilities that has gone undetected and therefore unmet and unchallenged, particularly in a formal school setting. In either case, additional testing and evaluation need to be carried out to determine which range of scores is most valid.

INTELLIGENCE: WHAT IS IT?

The word "intelligence" is so frequently used by both professionals and laymen that its meaning is taken for granted, couched somewhere in the context of how it is used. However, it is not a concept that is easy to define. Even among professionals, there is no single definition that explains the "attributes" of intelligence. This is because the word "intelligence" is a noun—a part of speech used to signify a thing or object having definite characteristics or descriptors. Intelligence is a highly complex or abstract "thing" for which there are no such definite attributes as long or short, red or green, light or heavy. When intelligence is studied or measured, what actually is observed is intelligent behavior or intelligent performance, not intelligence *per se*.

If we think in terms of intelligent behavior, rather than intelligence, it is easier to identify and build a basis for

ACTOR A   ACTOR B

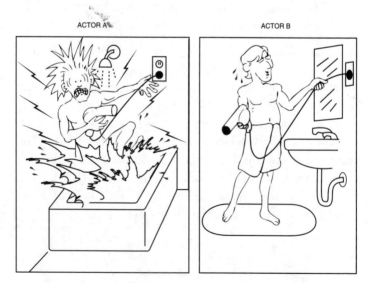

defining the abstract concept. For example, of the above two behaviors, check the one which you think is more intelligent.

Of course you checked the panel showing Actor B, whose behavior is far more intelligent than that of Actor A. You compared one behavior to a related behavior under the same set of circumstances. In order to do this, you had to have a basic storehouse of information about electricity, its nature, and its relationship to water. The process you went through to make an observation and judgment of intelligent behavior should in itself give you some insight into the nature of intelligent behavior.

The basis of intelligent behavior must be some kind of knowledge and information in its broadest sense. This information may have been acquired formally or informally. For example, if Actor A were only two years old, the behavior shown would not be considered unintelligent on the part of the child. (We might question the intelligence of the parent who permitted the child to be in a position to act dangerously and without the information on which to act intelligently.)

The impact of intelligence upon intelligent behavior begins with memory. For instance, in the preceding example, information about electricity and the dangers of mixing electricity with water must be remembered in order to affect behavior.

A factor related to remembering information is the application of previous learning to current situations. This is the ability to transfer or to generalize. Some individuals have much more capacity for transfer than do others. Persons well-endowed with this ability are usually found to be significantly more intelligent than those who do not possess a high degree of this ability.

Other facets of intelligence and intelligent behavior include speed in arriving at answers and solutions as well as problem-solving ability. To arrive at a solution, a person must identify the problem, analyze it, think of alternatives, apply previous knowledge, make a decision, and offer a solution. The entire act involves integration—putting it all together with balance and efficiency.

This essentially summarizes the nature of intelligent behavior. Intelligence tests try to measure intelligence by setting up situations and observing intelligent behavior. The tests use different kinds of questions and problems requiring the application of related and overlapping abilities. The various specialized tasks of the intelligence tests require an interplay of overall general ability and specific abilities in varying degrees. Intelligence tests must include a wide variety of question types in order to come up with a single score. As we continue to use the term "intelligence" in this context, it is important to understand that we are really only able to observe and discuss intelligent behavior and intelligent performance. From these observations, we extrapolate intelligence.

The study and identification of attributes of intelligence as reflected through intelligent behavior began in the 19th century. Herbert Spencer, who wrote *The Principles of Psychology* (1855), and Sir Frances Galton, whose work *Hereditary Genius* (1870) is a classic in the field, both believed in a general factor of intelligence related to but more important than other specific abilities. This theory was statistically confirmed by Charles Spearman, a pioneer in the statistical study of intelligence. Spearman's major works are *The Nature of Intelligence and the Principles of Cognition* (1923) and *Abilities of Man, Their Nature and Measurement* (1932). Spearman developed the statistical method of factor analysis, applied it to the results of intelligence tests, and concluded that there are two factors in intelligence, *g* and *s*. General ability, or *g*, is pervasive in all kinds of tasks and is therefore most important. Specific, or *s* factors, are part of intelligent behaviors, but intelligence *per se* is characterized by a general way of behaving that equally affects all kinds of tasks.

The lack of agreement among researchers in the field is clearly seen by comparing Spearman's theory to that of another researcher, L.L. Thurstone, who, in *Multiple Factor Analysis: A Development and Expansion of the Vectors of Mind* (1924), identified seven basic abilities as being part of a "simple structure." These abilities were: spatial, perceptual, numeric, verbal meaning, verbal fluency, memory, and inductive reasoning. He later identified an eighth, motor ability, in very young children. But he did not believe that there was an all-pervasive general factor involved.

Other researchers confirmed the existence of a general factor but found that it was not equally essential in the performance of all kinds of tasks. As a result, it has been proposed that there are intermediary group factors and also more specific abilities that relate and overlap in terms of application to the intelligent performance of tasks.

In addition, J.P. Guilford, in his work on the structure of the intellect, has proposed the existence of three large groups of abilities and 120 interrelating specific abilities. These are but a few of the researchers' theories about intelligence and its makeup. They summarize the major areas of both controversy and agreement among professionals in the field.

Although there is no consensus on a specific definition of intelligence, there are many areas of agreement about the general nature of intelligence. These are confirmed by the high correlation of the results from different intelligence tests.

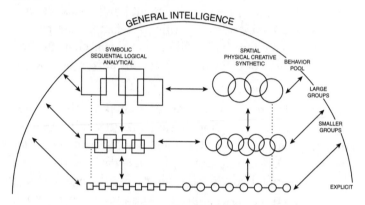

IDEAL MODEL

Interacting Structure of Intelligent Human Behaviors

First, there is a general intelligence ability that is used for various tasks and problems. This general ability or behavior is more critical in certain kinds of situations than in others. Further, there are secondary or group behaviors which are used in many situations, though they are not as pervasive as the general intelligence behavior. In addition, a larger set of smaller and more specific abilities comes into play in certain kinds of tasks. The general factor, large group behaviors, small group behaviors, and specific abilities overlap, interrelate, and interact. Most tasks with which a person is confronted tap more than one ability or behavior.

Whether behaviors are general, group, or specific, the behaviors and abilities referred to are mental or cognitive abilities. They relate to the functioning of the human brain.

Intelligence tests are, in one sense, a method of measuring this mental capacity, and differences in I.Q. scores are indicative of differences in brain structure as well as of differences that arise from exposure and experience.

BRAIN FUNCTION: CREATIVITY AND INTELLIGENCE

In recent years research on the difference between left-brain and right-brain functions has cast new light on mental processes and on the relationship between intelligence and creativity. Traditionally, the left hemisphere of the brain has been referred to as the dominant hemisphere and the right hemisphere as the minor hemisphere. However, it is now believed that the dominance of one hemisphere over another is essentially the result of learning and mental exercise, not an inherent quality.

The difference between left- and right-brain functions is qualified by the mental activities that are processed in each half of the brain. The left hemisphere is the control center for such intellectual functions as memory, language, logic, computation, seriation, classification, writing, analysis, and convergent thinking. This encompasses the traditional skills and abilities necessary for academic success. It is the left-brain functions that are the primary skills of importance in tests of intelligence.

The right hemisphere is the control center for the mental functions involved in intuition, extrasensory perception, attitudes and emotions, visual and spatial relationships, music, rhythm, dance, physical coordination and activity, synthesis, and divergent thinking processes. Wolfgang Luthe in *Creativity Mobilization Technique* (1976) characterizes left-brain thinking as "spotlight" thinking and right-brain thinking as "floodlight" thinking. This is a most picturesque, succinct, and accurate description of the difference between the two.

The functions of the left brain are characterized by sequence and order in comparison to the functions of the right brain, which are characterized as holistic and diffuse. The left brain can put the parts together into an organized whole; the right brain instinctively sees the whole, then the parts. Left-brain thinking is the essence of academic success and intelligence as it is currently measured; right-brain thinking is the essence of creativity. The two hemispheres must function in a balanced and integrated manner for wholesome human functioning to occur and for mental and physical health to be likewise in balance.

We live in a "left-brain" society, and nowhere is this more emphasized than in the schools. Schools are almost wholly oriented to the promotion and glorification of left-brain mental activity at the expense of the development of those activities which are right-brain functions. Thus, those individuals who are dominantly right-brain thinkers are out of tune to the drum-beat of most classroom and community settings. This is limiting not only to the youngsters who learn and express themselves through the creative, spatial, visual, physical, and holistic processes but also to the left-brain thinkers who have a large region of mental and physical functioning which goes undeveloped and unchallenged due to lack of exercise and practice.

Highly creative and highly intelligent individuals function with good balance in development and interaction between the two halves of the brain. In fact, creativity cannot occur in a vacuum; one must have information to draw upon from the left-brain abilities in order to act creatively.

This raises an intriguing possibility that the general factor of intelligence, which is so complex and difficult to define, may somehow be related to the integrated speed, efficiency, and flexibility of interaction between the left- and right-brain functions.

Following is a simple summary of some very complex information. It shows the principle of a general rule of brain activity. In actuality, it has been shown that there are small or minor areas in both hemispheres that are capable of carrying on the activities generally centered in the opposite half. For example, some language activity may be centered in the right brain; some visual-spatial activity may be centered in the left brain. In addition, the functions are generally reversed in a few individuals where the holistic type of thinking is controlled by the right hemisphere. This reversal of function seems more likely to be present in persons who are neither right- nor left-hand dominant—persons described as ambidextrous. On the whole, however, the general rule of differentiation of function applies.

A child who appears less intelligent than others on the basis of traditional tests and who has difficulty learning in a regular classroom may well be a visual-spatial, holistic learner rather than a slow learner. This is most likely to be true if the youngster shows evidence of good mental agility and ability when dealing with problems that require physical action or the manipulation of objects, rather than ideas, for a solution. Such a child may well be functionally handicapped in a schoolroom where instruction must be given in a form that requires the child to use the dominant left-brain mental processes. Such a child will not only have difficulty with traditional instruction but will also experience frustration when the majority of learning is based solely on mastery

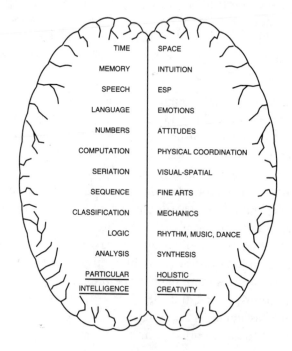

Mental and Physical Health

INTELLIGENT CREATIVITY-CREATIVE INTELLIGENCE

Left-Brain, Right-Brain Mental Activities

of written and spoken language. This frustration will further add to the difficulty in learning as the child begins to view himself or herself as a person who cannot succeed. Continually lower scores on intelligence tests will accompany the frustration-failure syndrome and lack of learning experienced by the youngster.

I.Q. TEST ANALYSIS: LEFT-BRAIN, RIGHT-BRAIN ABILITIES

Now that you have been introduced to the concept of right-brain and left-brain, you are probably very curious about where you fit in. The I.Q. test you took at the beginning of the book taps both left-brain and right-brain abilities.

You may have done extremely well on one type of question, but not so well on the other. Most people will find one type of question easier, but will have abilities in both areas. As noted in an earlier section of this book, it is not possible to construct a paper-and-pencil test which comprehensively tests the right-brain types of abilities. However, while most paper-and-pencil I.Q. tests are essentially tests of left-brain functions, each specific item in the test can be analyzed for its left-brain, right-brain components, and from this analysis some very interesting conclusions may be drawn.

We have carefully analyzed each specific question on your I.Q. test and have placed each into one of two categories. The first category contains those questions that test predominantly left-brain functions; the second category contains those questions that test both left- and right-brain functions. By identifying those questions which required right-brain processing on your part, you may gain further insight into your own I.Q. score.

Return now to your I.Q. test and, on the analysis sheet on page 76, list under Category I the left-brain questions that you missed and under Category II the right-brain questions that you got wrong. Then carefully review *all* the questions from *both* categories that you had *correct* and in the last column list those questions from among your correct answers that were "just right guesses." By comparing these three columns, we can come to a number of conclusions:

1. If you missed a fairly equal number of items from both those itemized as left-brain and those characterized as right-brain, then the possibility is that there is a dominance of neither right- nor left-brain processing. In other words, you employ a balanced left- and right-brain processing in most problems and questions that you encounter.

2. If most of the questions that you missed fall into the second category (questions requiring right-brain processing), then the probability is that you are a left-brain oriented individual who tends to approach and answer problems and questions primarily through left-brain processing.

3. If most of the questions that you missed are under the left-brain category, it may indicate that you are primarily or dominantly a right-brain thinker. If you did quite well on the questions which are based on or require right-brain skills but did not score particularly high on the test, you may very well be a very intelligent right-brain thinker. An in-depth individual test which is professionally administered and which includes the "performance" type of questions and problems would give you a better analysis of your abilities and of your I.Q.

4. Take another look at the number of questions at which you guessed but which you answered correctly. These answers were arrived at through intuitive thinking, which is a *right-brain* process. It is most likely, especially

if there are several of these, that they were not wild guesses but were arrived at through the right-brain intuitive function's interacting at an unconscious level with information stored deep in the left-brain memory bank. These answers, regardless of the category of the questions, are indicative of right-brain functioning.

Category I: Left-Brain Questions

1. Primarily a left-brain question that taps abilities in sequencing and analysis. It also requires the right-brain ability to recognize position in space.

2. A left-brain question tapping abilities in classification, analysis, general information, and memory.

5. A left-brain question requiring mathematical and sequencing skills.

6. A left-brain question tapping classification, memory, analysis, and general informational abilities.

7. A left-brain question requiring information, memory, analysis, and general informational abilities.

8. A left-brain question tapping classification, memory, information, and analysis skills.

10. A left-brain question tapping ability in logic and analysis.

11. A left-brain question requiring mathematical, informational, and memory skills.

13. A left-brain question requiring logic and analysis.

16. A left-brain question requiring numerical, mathematical, informational, memory, and analysis skills.

17. A left-brain question tapping classification, information, and memory.

18. A left-brain question requiring language and analysis skills.

20. A left-brain question tapping mathematical, informational, memory, and analysis skills.

*22. A left-brain question requiring language, information, and memory. However, if you arrived at the answer through a mental picture of the garden where these vegetables grow, you are relying on right-brain processing in problem solving.

23. A left-brain question tapping classification, information, memory, analysis, and analogy.

24. A left-brain question requiring numerical and mathematical skills, information, and memory.

*26. A left-brain question in logic and analysis. However, if you arrived at an answer by using a pictorial diagram, you are relying to a great extent on right-brain information processing.

28. A left-brain question requiring mathematical and analysis skills along with memory and general information.

29. A left-brain question tapping language, general information, memory, and classification.

30. A left-brain question tapping information, memory, analysis, and classification skills.

32. A left-brain question tapping mathematical, informational, memory, sequencing, and analysis skills.

33. A left-brain question requiring language, information, classification, analysis, and memory skills.

34. A left-brain question requiring language, information, memory, classification, and analysis.

35. A left-brain question tapping language, classification, and analysis skills.

36. A left-brain question tapping mathematical, informational, memory, and analysis skills.

38. A left-brain question tapping language, sequencing, informational, memory, and classification skills. The right-brain position-in-space function is also related.

39. A left-brain question requiring mathematical, memory, and informational and analysis skills.

41. A left-brain question requiring language, classification, and analysis skills.

43. A left-brain question requiring language, information, sequencing, and analysis skills. The right-brain function of position-in-space also comes into play.

44. A left-brain skill requiring mathematical, informational, memory, sequencing, and analysis skills.

45. A left-brain question tapping information, memory, classification, and analysis abilities.

48. A left-brain question requiring logic and analysis skills.

50. A left-brain question tapping language, memory, and analysis abilities.

52. A left-brain question requiring language, information, memory, classification, and analysis skills.

53. A left-brain question tapping language, information, memory, classification, and analysis skills.

55. A left-brain question tapping mathematical, informational, memory, and analysis skills.

56. A left-brain question tapping logic and analysis skills.

58. A left-brain question tapping language, information, classification, memory, and analysis abilities.

60. A left-brain question tapping language, classification, information, memory, and analysis abilities.

Category II: Right-Brain Questions

3. A right-brain question based on ability to see relationships in space and form. It also requires left-brain skills in classification.

4. This question taps both the right-brain skills in space and form and left-brain number skills.

9. A right-brain question requiring ability in space and form, but also requiring left-brain skills in classification and analogy.

12. A right-brain question tapping abilities in space and form, but also requiring left-brain skills in classification and analysis.

14. A right-brain question tapping abilities in space-form relationships, but also requiring left-brain skills in classification and analysis.

15. A question tapping the right-brain abilities in spatial relationships but also requiring left-brain analysis and sequencing.

19. A question that is right-brain in terms of the information with which it deals but left-brain in that it taps abilities in vocabulary, analogy, and analysis.

21. A right-brain question dealing with space and form relationships, but also requiring left-brain abilities of analysis and analogy.

*22. A left-brain question requiring language, information, and memory. However, if you arrived at the answer through a mental picture of the garden where these vegetables grow, you are relying on right-brain processing in problem solving.

25. A right-brain question tapping abilities in space-form relationships which also requires left-brain skills of classification and analysis.

*26. A left-brain question in logic and analysis. However, if you arrived at an answer by using a pictorial diagram, you are relying to a great extent on right-brain information processing.

27. A right-brain question tapping space and form relationships, but also requiring left-brain numerical skills.

31. A right-brain question tapping informational, memory, analysis, and classification skills.

37. A right-brain question tapping abilities in space-form relationships and requiring left-brain classification and analysis.

40. A right-brain question tapping space-form relationship abilities and requiring left-brain skills in classification and analysis.

42. A combination of right- and left-brain skills. The question is based on ability to gain information through visual images but requires the left-brain functions of information, memory, classification, and analysis.

46. A right-brain question requiring abilities in space-form relationships, but also requiring left-brain skills in numbers.

47. A right-brain question requiring abilities in spatial relationships, but also requiring left-brain number skills.

49. A right-brain question requiring abilities in space and form relationships, but also tapping left-brain numerical skills and abilities in classification and analysis.

51. A right-brain question tapping space-form relationship skills, but also requiring left-brain abilities in classification, numbers, and analysis.

54. A question based on ability to process right-brain visual-image information but requiring left-brain information, classification, and analysis skills.

57. A question that taps right-brain position-in-space abilities but which is heavily left-brain in requiring language, information, memory, sequencing, and analysis skills.

59. A question that deals with right-brain position-in-space skills but which also requires left-brain language, sequencing, and information and analysis skills.

The foregoing analysis of left- and right-brain functioning raises some interesting points.

The questions on the I.Q. test that tap right-brain functions also require abilities which are essentially left-brain. However, *the reverse is not true*. Most left-brain questions on the test which deal with language and numbers do not necessarily require right-brain abilities.

We are thus able to identify and separate the questions into two different categories.

Right-brain thinkers, when confronted with questions of language, logic, or mathematics—which are essentially left-brain problems—may use pictures or diagrams or may think in mental pictures in an effort to solve them. Or they "guess"—which is an intuitive, right-brain response.

In brief, they are applying right-brain processing to left-brain questions. Thus, the list of correct "guesses" on the test is a further strong indication of right-brain functioning.

Although the analysis is far from precise, it will give you a good indication of whether you employ balanced or predominantly left- or right-brain processing in your approach to the problems confronting you in your everyday life.

Such insight might well be significant. If, for example, the indication is that you are predominantly left-brain oriented, perhaps you are overlooking or neglecting the development of some creative or artistic talent which you may possess.

If the indications are that you are predominantly right-brain oriented, then you are essentially a creative individual who tends to think holistically or in patterns and who may, therefore, have encountered past difficulties in a left-brain-oriented society.

LEFT-BRAIN, RIGHT-BRAIN TEST ANALYSIS

Category I Left-Brain	Category II Right-Brain	Guesses

CREATIVITY

Although the intelligence required for traditional academic success is generally the result of mental activity peculiar to left-brain processing, the creativity of open and original production is the result of mental activity peculiar to right-brain processing. The first is sequentially ordered, analytical, logical, and temporal; the second is intuitive, diffuse, and spatial. The left-brain process allows the carefully ordered building of a whole from its many parts. The right-brain process allows an almost intuitive grasping of the whole in relationship to its parts.

Creativity was once thought of as a process or activity that was unique to production and performance in art, music, and drama. Creative production and performance exist, however, in all areas of human endeavor. These include not only the visual and performing arts, but also the academic disciplines, the professions, government and politics, and so on. The creative producer or performer is one who brings innovation and new life-forms into any field of human activity: the scientist who discovers a new vaccine; the coach who invents a new offensive tactic; the businessperson who creates a new and needed service; the researcher who develops a new theory about human behavior—all such activities and more are examples of creative endeavor in areas outside the visual and performing arts.

Creativity requires individuality, independence of thought and action, spontaneity, originality, and flexibility of action combined with dedication to purpose. It is more than spontaneous, original, flexible, and independent thought, however. Although this type of thinking is essential and can occur only where there is a free and unencumbered flow of ideas, images, and emotions, such ideas and thoughts cease to be spontaneous and original after a period of time elapses subsequent to their emergence. In addition to creative thinking, creativity involves a sense of purpose coupled with action. The creative act requires that emerging ideas and thoughts be organized into new or different patterns from their previous organization. The creative act has a result—a product, material, service, or mental structure. This result, in order to meet the criteria of creativity, must be different from similar previous structures.

All humans possess the ability to create or to be creative. For many persons this innate creative ability is squelched before they even enter school, or, if not by that time, then shortly thereafter. This is because of the cultural-social emphasis upon conformity, acceptance, doing the "right" thing, finding the "correct" answer. Some creative ability can be recaptured later on, even in adulthood, but once the individual has learned to suppress the basic and necessary mental and personality activities of the creative process, the chances are slim for later development of full potential.

All human beings possess creative ability, but not all possess the creative talent of a Beethoven, Picasso, Einstein, or Edison. There is a difference between ordinary and super creativity. This difference is not really a difference in the process; rather, it represents different points on a continuum of ability or talent. For example:

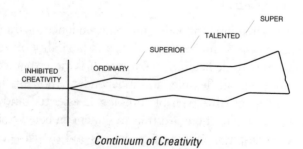

Continuum of Creativity

There are tests available for the measurement of creativity, but the results that are generated are not mathematically specific as they are with intelligence tests. Levels of creative talent cannot be broken down into specific levels of performance or potential but might be viewed as a surging and churning ocean current whose visible peaks are manifest in the ebb and flow of magnificent, unrestricted waves breaking in toward a distant and undefined shore.

Tests of creativity provide questions and problems for which there are no "best" or "right" answers. Their purpose is the testing of divergent thinking styles. Among the types of questions used on such tests are the following.

1. **The Untitled Story:** A short, one-paragraph story is presented and the individual is asked to suggest titles for it. The question is scored on the basis of: a) quantity—the number of titles offered; and b) quality—the originality or uniqueness of the title suggestions. For example:

Write newspaper headlines for this story:

Jake Rush, a local private eye, was found today crushed by a grease pit hoist in an abandoned Pittman Street garage. Jake's body was found stuffed in a large plastic bag. Jake had apparently been attempting to escape since he had poked a hole in the bag. Clutched in his hand were the dusty remnants of the jewels recently stolen from the internationally renowned Groist Ltd. diamond firm. Mr. Rush had been hired by the insurance agency of Crouch, Inc. to assist in the investigation and recovery of the stolen jewels. Detectives theorized that Rush tried to single-handedly apprehend the criminals in their hideaway and was overpowered from behind. The jewels had apparently been stashed in a hole at the bottom of the pit, and Rush found them just before his untimely end. There is a question as to whether Rush's estate will receive the recovery reward.

Examples of Ordinary Titles: "Private Eye Found Dead"; "Detective Crushed by Hoist"; "Jake Rush Killed by Thieves"

Examples of Creative Titles: "Rush Crushed"; "Ouch-Pouch End for Crouch P.I."; "Groist Wiped Out by Hoist"; "Drastic Plastic Reward"

2. **The Untitled Cartoon or Caricature:** Scored in the same way as the untitled story.

Ordinary Captions: "Help!" "Don't just stand there!"

Creative Captions: "Give my regards to Broadway!" "Quick! Call 855-3267 and ask if John Smith's life insurance premium has been paid!"

3. **Paired Words**: Pairs of words that appear to have no relationship to each other are presented. The individual is asked to name a third word that is somehow related or common to the other two. For example:

sugar:	walking	*(cane)*
bank:	story	*(teller)*
eye:	meow	*(cat's)*
day:	pipe	*(dream)*

This type of question has obvious limitations. Suggested answers are available. If the scorer is not creative enough to recognize the validity of unnamed possibilities, the question-type fails as a test of creativity and becomes a test of convergent thinking ability.

4. **Visual Fill-In:** Partly completed pictures or designs are presented. The individual might be asked to give as many interpretations as possible of what the design might represent, be, or become. For example:

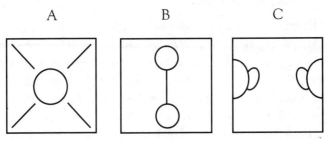

A   B   C

This question is scored on the basis of quantity and uniqueness of answers.

Examples of Ordinary Answers: A. sun; B. barbell; C. two cup handles

Examples of Creative Answers: A. four-legged spider; inside of a well; spaceship, front or rear view; intersection with round, fat crossing guard; B. door handle; two knotholes hooked together by crack; stereo headset; two floating balloons; part of a necklace; old-fashioned telephone earpiece; C. two clowns whispering; two rabbits going in opposite directions; mirror image of left ear; mirror image of right ear; ludicrous freeway loops

Note that the creative answers are more than unique and original; they exhibit richness and fluency of both thought and language.

5. **Object Uses:** Subject is given an example of an ordinary object and asked to name as many different uses for the object as possible. For example, the object might be a pencil. The common answer would be to use for writing or drawing. Creative answers would include such things as: houseplant stake; back-scratcher; string-holder, and so on.

These are a few examples of the types of questions used in tests of creativity. Some of the limitations of such tests are obvious. First is the time required for scoring, which is extensive. Second, the creativity of the test designer will place both upper and lower limits on the levels of creativity taken into account. Third, the creativity of the test scorer is critical. The scorer must be able to recognize the validity of relationships and possibilities that are not offered in the suggested guidelines for scoring.

There is a more simple and effective method for determining the possibilities for creativity of an individual: the observation of the person's behavior over a period of time. One must first identify some of the behaviors that indicate creative potential and performance. Among these are a prolific quantity of ideas along with uniqueness of ideas. Other behaviors include: independence and individuality in thought and action; curiosity; originality; self-assertiveness; fluency; process (rather than product) orientation; sensitivity to beauty; sensitivity to emotions (one's own and those of others); self-honesty; willingness to take risks; willingness to be different; self-motivation; unusual and active imagination; ability to live with uncertainty; adaptability and flexibility; intuition; persistence; production of innovative ideas and things; a keen and sometimes unusual sense of humor.

Logical thinking and analysis can be performed on schedule. Creativity cannot. In the creative process there is first a period of readiness or openness. This may involve the acquisition of information and ideas, studying or identifying a problem, and constructing some sort of hypothesis. Readiness is followed by a sort of incubation period in which the individual mulls over, lives with, and thinks about possibilities for new organization. Sometimes during incubation insight occurs. Insight may come after a few hours or days, or it might take months or even years. This is the part of the creative process that cannot be forced. It is depicted in cartoons as a light bulb's being suddenly turned on inside a person's head, and this is probably the most succinct and vivid description of what happens when all the possibilities have been synthesized into a new organization or problem solution. After that, it is a matter of producing the actual result and then perhaps testing it out to see if it works as imagined.

Creativity and the creative process cannot be rushed, and there are no magic limits on the various stages. A stage might take minutes or years. Creative people are noted, however, for persistence. They will persist toward a goal with great flexibility but also with commitment. It is this persistence that represents the significant difference between the productively creative individual and the simple original thinker or idea generator.

Intelligence and intelligent capabilities are necessary for creativity to result in "good" products. The creative mind must have information, ideas, and concepts from which to draw. Although highly creative people do not necessarily show high I.Q. scores, they would not be capable of creative endeavor as described here if their intelligence capabilities were extremely low. When reference is made to "highly intelligent, highly creative" persons, the reference is to individuals who are highly creative and who have actual, though unregistered, I.Q.s of 140 to 150 or even above. Experience shows that a majority of unusually creative persons tend to score between 120 and 139 on standard intelligence tests. Whether such persons are more creative than intelligent or whether they score lower on convergent types of intelligence tests because they are divergent types of thinkers is a question that cannot be answered.

ARE INTELLIGENCE SCORES USEFUL AND IMPORTANT?

For a long time there has been a great deal of controversy among educators and parents over the use of intelligence scores and their validity. Too often, children have been incorrectly labeled as having less ability and/or potential than they actually possess, and they have been placed in very limiting educational settings as a result. It is not only the placement that is a tragedy in such a case; it is the predictive factor of future success and basic underlying attitudes toward self that are extremely destructive. Unfortunately, it is true that human beings tend to fulfill the prophecies made on their behalf.

The controversy, however, is not over the use of intelligence tests but over their *misuse*. Any long-term decisions about a child's educational needs or placement in the educational setting should take into consideration a series of I.Q. scores along with a host of other behaviors that are not and cannot be identified through such tests.

A low score on an intelligence test may signal that a child needs different methods of instruction. A learning-disabled child, for example, who does not receive early and sound remedial assistance and concrete forms of instruction in school will very likely show a test pattern of decreasing test scores between entering school and arriving at about a sixth-grade or 12- or 13-year-old level. The child may be quite intelligent, but because of poor language and math skills he or she will increasingly appear to learn like a slow learner and test like a slow learner. Recent trends toward main-streaming all children should be helpful in reducing such educational travesties, particularly when different kinds of instruction and instructional media are made available to learners whose needs are different from those of the other students.

Another swirl of controversy over the use of intelligence tests revolves around the possibility of "cultural bias." Cultural bias refers to the possibility that a test may be appropriate only for individuals whose backgrounds have prized, promoted, and/or taught certain skills. For example, traditional intelligence tests assumed thinking skills and language skills that a person would acquire from an average, English-speaking middle-class background. A person for whom English was a second language and/or whose cultural environment stressed different values would be laboring under a handicap in trying to answer the traditional questions that were asked. Most tests today have been rewritten in attempts to eliminate such bias. An important point to emphasize here is that even though a test may indeed be culturally biased and therefore not give the best indication of "intelligence," the results from intelligence tests are generally quite accurate in predicting future success in the school situation as schools are presently structured. This leads to the next point—that along with further research and effort to develop truly culture-free tests the real problem may need to be addressed within the structure of the schools.

In spite of the controversy over intelligence tests, it has been shown that the results give a good indication not only of a child's probable future success in school but also of future success as an adult. The classic long-term study of about 1500 highly intelligent schoolchildren which was begun in 1921 by Lewis M. Terman, and published in 1926 and later as the *Genetic Studies of Genius* series, has resulted in some very significant and interesting information along this line. This study has observed the individuals identified in 1921 as highly intelligent over a period of many years and at different checkpoints throughout their adulthood. Although the study will not be complete until after the year 2000, the results to date show that these individuals, with few exceptions, have achieved significant rewards and recognition, have an unusually high degree of success professionally and financially, and enjoy better health and longer lifespans than their less gifted contemporaries. All in all, the highly intelligent have proved by behavior and performance to be outstanding in achievement, educational levels, contributions to society, career success, and health compared to others less gifted.

The final philosophical area of controversy over intelligence tests rests on the conviction of many people that it is inappropriate to try to specifically measure something that cannot be specifically defined. Indeed, the concept of intelligence is a very complex and abstract idea over which even professionals do not fully share a consensus of opinion in the matter of definition. Alfred Binet, the "father" of intelligence tests and the author of the 1905 *Binet Intelligence Scale*, was a Paris psychologist of the late 19th and early 20th centuries who was given the task of finding a way to identify children in the Paris schools who were not able to handle regular schoolwork and to learn in a traditional classroom setting. In an attempt to identify such handicapped learners, Binet began identifying the skills and abilities that were necessary for children of different ages to succeed in school. He then developed a test based upon samples of questions and problems that children who can learn successfully should be able to complete. This was the first I.Q. test, and its purpose was to identify handicapped learners. When Binet was asked, however, what intelligence is, he replied by saying that it is what his test measures. This may seem like a ludicrous definition, but it is actually the key to a basis for defining intelligence—a way of performing or behaving.

Not only did Binet define intelligence as what his test measured, but he further suggested that it was more fruitful to set about the task of measuring and studying it than to engage in academic arguments relative to its definition. Other prominent researchers have attempted both, and a look at some of their definitions will provide some insight into our definition of intelligence.

Terman described it as "the ability to carry on abstract thinking"; Woodrow, another of the early analyzers of intelligence, as "the capacity to acquire capacity"; Thurstone, in his 1924 *The Nature of Intelligence*, as "the capacity to live a trial-and-error existence with alternatives which are not yet complete." (This alludes to aspects of creative behavior.) Wechsler, developer of the "Wechsler Intelligence Scale" and author of *Measurement and Appraisal of Adult Intelligence* (1972), defined it as "the aggregate or global capacity to act purposefully, to think rationally, and to deal effectively with [the] environment."

Other definitions imply speed, efficiency, and innate ability or potential. All of these are partly correct. Intelligence, as described here, is reflected in *human* behavior. While some animals may be taught specific abilities, such as "fetching" or "prancing" or "balancing a ball" or finding the way through a maze, few if any animals would "score" well on a general intelligence test. Intelligence, in a sense, separates humans from other forms of animal life. Some humans have more intelligence than others. Some have different kinds of intelligence. However, *intelligence in general is characterized by a mental process that incorporates speed, efficiency, agility, and flexibility in the purposeful mental activity of dealing with life tasks, problem solving, and the production of both conventional and innovative ideas, services, and products. It requires not only the ability to apply attained skills but also the ability to acquire new ones.*

Intelligence tests, although accurate in the type of predictions that they can support, do have limitations. They measure intelligence only as defined by convergent, as opposed to divergent, ways of thinking. Convergent thinking is the kind of mental process used to arrive at answers which are predetermined—the best or right answer in a given set of circumstances. This kind of thinking and approach to problem solving is the one predominantly fostered in schools and the one prized in many families. It is the kind of thought process used to answer conventional multiple-choice or true-false types of questions; it is the type of thought process used to determine the types of values to be applied when concerning oneself about "what other people will think." It is closed and not very dynamic, although in logical and analytical applications it can pose high challenges. It is the type of thinking that largely comprises measured intelligence.

Divergent thought, on the other hand, is characterized by openness and the production of unique and original answers and solutions. It is the thought process associated with creativity, individuality, and difference. While prized in some families and in a few educational settings, it goes relatively unreinforced and unnurtured in our society.

The inability of intelligence tests to measure or require the application of divergent thinking behavior—along with schooling's emphasis upon convergent types of thinking and abstract, verbal, and sequential methods of presenting learning material—often stands in the way of identifying intelligence and giftedness in individuals who are not convergent types of thinkers. History confirms the misinterpretation and misunderstanding of the abilities of certain individuals who have proven to be highly gifted and talented and even of genius stature as adults.

For example, Hermann von Helmholtz, whose contributions in the fields of physics and mathematics were gigantic in nature, did not do well or impress his teachers while a student. Although extremely talented in mathematics, other school tasks of a routine and convergent nature did not allow him the independence of thought necessary for creative endeavor. He spent his time daydreaming, thinking through ideas of interest to him, and paying little attention to required schoolwork.

Noted poet Ralph Waldo Emerson graduated in the bottom half of his class. Thomas Edison was told that he was too stupid to learn. Albert Einstein did not talk until he was three years old and learned to read much later than most children. He did very poorly in school. John B. Watson, noted psychologist, was described by teachers as lazy and insubordinate. Eleanor Roosevelt was viewed by teachers as having few redeeming qualities. She was looked upon as a withdrawn daydreamer who came out of her shell only during selfish attempts to be the center of attention. Ludwig von Beethoven's music teacher considered him a washout as a composer. Jan Masaryk, while visiting the United States as a child, was labeled retarded on the basis of one I.Q. test and was briefly institutionalized as a result.

These are but a few examples of the inappropriate evaluations of highly intelligent, creative, and divergent thinkers who were believed to have little or no ability because they were *different*. All can be identified as basically creative, individualistic, highly intelligent persons who did not fit into the classical convergent structure of the schools.

Such individuals as those noted above may be misevaluated for a number of reasons. They may be so highly intelligent that routine classroom learning is boring and dull. In their refusal to participate, they turn to daydreaming and/or unacceptable classroom behavior. They may also be highly creative instead of, or in addition to, being highly intelligent. Their thinking processes may not fit into traditional educational settings. They may often be infinitely more intelligent and/or creative than their teachers, who have little understanding of and empathy for their needs. They may have learning difficulties that interfere with their ability to learn in abstract and conventional ways. Or, the misevaluated student may be subjected to a test which is completely inappropriate because of language and cultural differences.

In any event, such children may be daydreamers, wisecrackers, or have other types of behavior problems. There are other reasons for youngsters to behave in ways that are not very acceptable to teachers, but the possibility of high intelligence and high creativity should never be overlooked.

CAN INTELLIGENCE BE IMPROVED OR RAISED?

Whether or not intelligence can be raised rests on whether general intelligence is inherited or learned. Which is the more important factor—heredity or environment? This has been a subject of controversy for many years.

Traditionally, on the basis of evidence of high intelligence and achievement in certain families, it was believed that intelligence was an inherited ability. However, with the growth and impact of knowledge accumulated in the behavioral and social sciences came an interest and belief in the importance of environment with respect to individual abilities and achievements. Volumes of research exist in support of both ideas, and controversy still surrounds the issue.

Common sense, however, dictates the importance and impact of both heredity and environment on both intelligence and achievement. Since the complexity of brain structure is related to intelligent behavior, obviously heredity is a factor. Think of brain structure and the complexity of neural connections as analogous to a network. It follows that the brain structure and capacity linked with high intelligence are like a highly developed urban network of freeways and their interchanges, while the brain structure associated with low intelligence is akin to a rural dirt crossroads. There is, then, some kind of innate potential which is inherited and which is related to the structure of the brain—the complexity of connections and its processing capabilities. In this sense, the upper limits of a person's intelligence are predetermined before birth. However, other factors—both physiological and environmental—do affect the development of intelligent capacity and intelligent capability.

First, the average person uses less than 15% to 20% of his or her total mental ability during a lifetime. This means that all persons have untapped mental resources that have never been developed and used.

Second, the first environment that a human occupies—the uterus—plays a significant part in the future development of intelligent capabilities. Conditions during pregnancy can seriously affect the development of the fetus in every way, including its brain and neural development. Lack of proper nutrition, intrauterine pressures, illness of the mother, physical and psychological trauma, parental chromosome damage as a result of drug use, and a host of other possibilities can damage the developing fetus and consequently place congenital limitations on an inherited brain structure.

Third, the home, the school, and the community environments of the developing child will also affect the development of potential mental abilities. Lack of love, lack of interaction with other people, and lack of nutritional foods can all inhibit the individual's intellectual and mental development. In reverse, an enriched and balanced environment can enhance and promote the development of mental abilities. In this sense, environment does have an effect upon intelligence as it is measured. But can intelligence be raised?

The answer to this is that every person does indeed possess an upper or outside limit of capability beyond which he or she cannot pass. However, since we know that the full mental capacity of the brain is never tapped, there are many things that can be done, particularly with children, to assist in the development and use of brain capacity.

The first environment is crucial. In order to ensure a healthy fetus and an uncomplicated birth, the mother needs to have the proper diet and to avoid the ingestion of drugs, alcohol, cigarette smoke, and other substances known to be potentially harmful to the developing fetus. Further, the pregnant woman should be under the care of a physician for the purpose of regular check-ups for weight control, body-fluid control, recommended regular exercise, and so on. It is also important that the mother be in good physical and mental health before the pregnancy occurs. These general guidelines are important not only for the health of the mother but as insurance that the unborn child has the best opportunity for normal and full development. The best sources for specific information are your physician and your local public health agency.

You can promote optimal mental development in a child from the earliest stages of infancy. Stimulate equal development of both hemispheres of the brain by changing the infant's position frequently so that he or she views the room from all angles. You want to avoid development of a superdominant hemisphere which might later inhibit interaction of the two hemispheres.

Talk to the developing infant. As the child begins to explore its environment through holding, touching, and pointing to objects, verbally identify the objects as "chair," "flower," etc. Constant exposure to language and its meaning helps to develop the child's verbal ability, a very important aspect of high intelligence.

Give the child warmth, love, and acceptance. Never spank or punish an infant for behavior you think is unacceptable. Babies have no concept of right or wrong and cannot even tell the difference between their own inside world and the outside world in general. Anger or harsh punishment can have no positive effects on infant behavior but can cause emotional distress that may result in high anxiety, uncertainty, and even lack of self-identity in the developing ego. On the contrary, babies must receive attention for attention's sake alone and must receive recognition for their accomplishments so that they do not develop the idea that misbehavior is the only way to get attention.

Provide the child with a nutritious, varied diet. Avoid excessive processed sugar. Processed sugar seems to be related to hyperactivity and decreased concentration in children. Although total prohibition is unnecessary in the normal, healthy child, limiting sweets is an easy way to eliminate sugar's interference in behavior and development. Common sense and balance are the keys to diet, along with any vitamin or mineral supplements that the child's doctor or clinic advises. A healthy, active mind must be housed in the healthy, active body of which it is a part.

Do not force the child to use one hand rather than the other. The child will probably show preference for either the left or right hand, and it is very important to balanced mental functioning that this natural dominance be honored.

Interference may result in the interruption of normal development of mental processing efficiencies that in turn can adversely affect the development of reading and writing skills.

Provide play objects appropriate to learning at the child's age level. Since young children learn through movement and manipulation, play activities must be appropriate to muscle development. Development progresses from large-muscle to smaller muscle to eye-hand coordination. Play objects that are inappropriate to developmental level will only frustrate enjoyment and learning. In other words, very small children should be encouraged to climb and tumble, then to construct with sturdy, large blocks long before they are expected to handle even large-piece picture puzzles. Play objects should also encourage the child to imagine and to pretend. Imaginative play is the basis for later symbolization in language development. Imaginative play also helps the development of the creative right-brain processes of the mind. Toys that do not have a specific, rigidly defined purpose are best. Certainly expensive toys are unnecessary; pots, pans, boxes, yarn balls, and such are all excellent play objects.

Encourage and provide opportunity for physical play and exercise. As a child grows from infancy into the preschool years, blocks, puzzles, crayons, and large picture books provide practice for small-muscle, eye-hand, creativity, and preconceptual development. Show the child a picture—something that relates to the child's level and experience—and have the child tell you what he or she thinks is happening, or make up a story about it, or name the colors or the objects, and so on. Help the child see more than what was originally obvious, but not lots more. Good learning and development occur in cupfuls, not large buckets.

Play word and imagination games with the child, such as:

1. Patty-cake and peek-a-boo with babies

2. Hide-and-seek with toddlers

3. "I'm thinking of something round in this room..." with 3- to 5-year-olds. Add to the complexity as the child becomes more agile and speedy in arriving at answers.

4. Play Twenty Questions with elementary school children. You have something in mind or a number in mind. The child gets to ask no more than twenty questions in trying to guess what it is. Young children will take wild guesses, but they will develop and can learn "strategies" for good questions. For example, if you are thinking of a number, they will learn to ask such things as: "Is it odd or even?"; "Is it under fifty?"; and so on.

5. Play the automobile plate game as a family game. How quickly can one think of a phrase to go with three license plate letters? For example: SUS—sit up straight; IWL—I want lunch. This type of game can become quite hilarious, alleviating the tedium of travel while developing speed, agility, and creativity of mental processes.

You must provide structure for the child of any age, but you must also allow for flexibility within that structure. Set standards of behavior, but then allow for creative solutions of problems and for understanding of gradations and shadings, not rigid dichotomies of right or wrong, good or bad, early or late. Promote reinforcement of new ideas and new concepts by suggesting that the child express a thought or idea through media other than the first one of presentation. Art, crafts, drama, mime, and song are all acceptable media for the reinforcement of learning.

Encourage creativity by prizing individuality, independence, and risk-taking. Discipline and tame that creativity by prizing sharing, cooperation, and personal responsibility.

And what about the adult I.Q.? The adult I.Q. is not as amenable to enhancement as that of a child. One reason is that the neural connections in the brain are pretty well complete by the age of 16 or 17. Another reason is that thinking and learning styles and attitudes are fairly well developed and are a part of the total personality by the time a person reaches adulthood. But, although I.Q. itself cannot be improved, level of performance is another matter. The fact that stroke victims who lose speech or partial control of their bodies can sometimes be retrained for effective functioning is a tribute to the undeveloped potential of the brain even in adults. The inherited level of intelligence cannot be increased in either child or adult, but the undeveloped and unused abilities within that inherited structure can be tapped, developed, and enhanced.

As an adult's life becomes more complex and more demanding, certain mental activities no longer become part of the daily routine. These can be resurrected and redeveloped with practice.

Puzzles provide a special kind of challenge and fascination and a painless route towards rekindling old skills and abilities. As skill with puzzles increases, proficiency with words, numbers, three-dimensional relationships, etc. may progress well beyond the peak reached during youth and the years of schooling. Crossword puzzles and other word puzzles are unparalleled aids for building vocabulary and word fluency; number puzzles serve to enhance skill at computation and calculation and to encourage successful recognition of relationships among numbers; jigsaw puzzles and three-dimensional puzzles expand the ability to visualize relationships in space. Increasing competence with one type of puzzle will not automatically make one more competent at another type of puzzle, but fascination with puzzles will lead the curious adult from one kind to the next, with consequent growth of abilities in other mental activities.

To improve your functional I.Q., the intelligence level at which you actually perform (not your measured I.Q.), you will find that reading and developing greater awareness of worlds other than your own is a superb mind-expanding activity. Read magazines and books, nonfiction and fiction, on topics of interest to you—travel, other cultures, art, archaeology, science, technology, etc. Read anything that provides new kinds of information and insights into life in general. Expanding your scope of interest and base of knowledge will not only increase your level of mental functioning but will make life more interesting and will make you more interesting as well.

Be positive. Use the "I can" rather than the "I can't" approach. Try, practice, develop a skill, ability, or interest to its fullest degree. Take the time to learn about or to learn how to do something that has been a secret ambition for a long time. One of the differences between the highly intelligent and the less intelligent is persistence and action. Intelligent, productive people are those who *do*, while others consider; they are people who try, while others give up; they are people who are willing to fail and try again, while others insist on first-time success.

Applying these ideas and principles will not turn you into a genius, unless you are a genius in disguise, but they will improve your attitudes, your general abilities, and your capacity for learning and will certainly make life more interesting and more personally satisfying.

PART III

Giftedness/Talent and Intelligence

RECOGNIZING GIFTEDNESS AND TALENT

Although the first intelligence tests were designed in an effort to identify youngsters who were mentally handicapped, the group of children around whom interest is currently focused is that of the gifted and talented. High intelligence test scores are but one of many indicators that a person has potential or demonstrated abilities that are clearly outstanding. A high I.Q. is an indication of giftedness and talent in academic and intellectual areas, but in addition to academic giftedness, there are other areas of human endeavor and accomplishment in which a person may also be gifted. This fact, which has long been recognized by people working with children, was significant in influencing the research and studies of creativity which began in the late 1950s and early 1960s.

A person may be gifted and talented in one or more of four areas. These are:

1. **Academic (intellectual intelligence):** The academically gifted person demonstrates outstanding potential and/or achievement in those areas which require mastery of a set of formalized symbols, such as language, or numbers, or both. This type of giftedness is reflected through I.Q. scores, subject area achievement scores, and academic or school marks.

2. **Creative:** The creatively gifted person demonstrates potential and/or achievement in those areas which require open, original, and uniquely productive thinking or action. Creativity can be demonstrated through the visual or performing arts, in academic areas,

business or politics, or in the social arena. There are tests which measure creativity, but, as previously stated, these have limitations, particularly in the difficulty of giving them to large groups of people. One of the best ways to identify creativity is on the basis of behaviors which indicate creative thinking and performance.

3. **Psychomotor (physical):** The physically gifted person demonstrates outstanding potential and/or performance in activities requiring large-muscle, small-muscle, and eye-hand coordination. These include such activities as sports, dance, mechanics, rhythm, and the skills required for mastering the use of fine arts media. Outstanding psychomotor abilities can also be measured on the basis of observation.

4. **Social/Personal/Leadership:** The person with a gift for leadership demonstrates outstanding potential and/or performance in the areas of social and personal abilities required for leadership. These abilities can be measured through observation of daily behavior and are based upon personality characteristics, communication abilities, and leadership skills.

I.Q. scores are not valid indicators of abilities in creative, psychomotor, and leadership areas. How, then, can individuals who are gifted in these areas be identified? The best way to positively identify these individuals is to observe their behavior on a regular basis and to keep a log of the incidence of behaviors which have over time been singled out as reliable indicators of giftedness and talent.

You can arrive at a fairly accurate idea of the extent of any person's giftedness and talent by observing the person's general behavior on a regular basis. In addition, there are certain behaviors exhibited by infants and preschool children that are indicators of general levels of intelligence. We can easily identify highly intelligent children by comparing their performance with average or expected levels of performance of members of the general population at the same age. The following case histories will give you an idea of the ways in which some giftedly intelligent and creative persons have behaved as children.

TERRI is now a young adult. She drank unassisted from a cup at the age of four months; cut her first teeth at five and one-half months; walked at 10 months; talked in simple sentences (one, two words) at 10 and one-half months. She dressed and undressed herself with equal ease by 14 months and was putting puzzles together and scribbling by the age of 18 months. She played cooperatively with other children the summer she was two. She was extremely social and competitive and was commonly the leader of the group.

Her outstanding physical coordination and willingness to take risks were apparent by age 18 months when she was found standing on top of the backyard swing set. Her mother gave her directions to help her get down, took her to the store and purchased sneakers, then showed her how to climb safely up and safely down. She could swim well by the age of three and a half.

Before entering kindergarten she composed lengthy and complicated stories and free-verse poetry and could add and subtract fractions in her head. Her individuality, willingness to take risks, conceptual maneuvers, and originality were highly encouraged by her family. She could write her name and numbers before entering school but was not taught to read. She was surrounded by and was exposed to a multitude of books and stories and was read to on a daily basis by her father and sometimes by her mother. The decision to not teach her to read was purposeful, as the school system she was entering was not prepared for a child who could already read at kindergarten entry.

As a fourth grader, Terri was the leader of a student protest against the teacher's methods of instruction. Her mother had discovered her at ten o'clock at night underneath her blankets with a flashlight writing spelling words ten times each. Surprised, because Terri was already reading above a tenth-grade level, her mother asked why Terri could not spell the words on the fourth-grade list. Terri informed her that she could indeed spell the words but that everyone had to write the words ten times whether they could spell them or not. Her mother reacted instantly with: "That's the dumbest thing I ever heard. Are you sure?" Terri was indeed sure, but was further informed to get her work done in the future before 10:00PM. A few days later Terri nonchalantly informed her mother that she had to stay after school. When asked why, she answered that there was a fourth-grade protest and the teacher had asked all the youngsters who were involved in signing the petition to come in after school. Terri had of course written the petition and elicited the signatures of most of the class. The petition said: "We think that we should not have to write our spelling words ten times each when we already know how to spell them, and my mother thinks it is dumb." It was signed by Terri and eighteen others. Terri won her case on the basis of the logic and procedures used. The teacher, who had never really thought about this traditional and foolish method of teaching spelling, decided that it was indeed "dumb" and agreed that words which could be spelled before the beginning of the unit did not have to be written ten times each.

Terri excelled academically until the fifth grade, when she explained at home that she had found it unrewarding to do all her work as fast and as well as she could because the teacher only gave her more of the same.

Terri's academic success in high school was not outstanding. She graduated at the bottom of the top third of her class, but excelled in sports, language-related subjects, and art. She also should have received a letter of commendation for sociability and personality. Her I.Q. has been tested as 150+, but she lost her interest in academic subjects at an early age because no real challenge was provided for her. Along with the development of some fine art skills, she also learned to play two musical instruments with highly competent, but not talented, performance.

Terri grew up in a family where there was high educational attainment, but where independence, individuality, and openness were prized over the conformity and social acceptance which are more likely to be valued in families of high academic achievers.

BETH reported having memories from the age of one. This is highly unusual in most individuals, even in highly sensitive and intelligent persons. She talked at an early age and could carry on a conversation with detail and fluency of language by age three. Her friends were usually older, and she was an accepted part of the adult world from a preschool age. Her powers of observation and memory were unique and her ability to group and classify as a preschooler was evidenced by the fact that she could identify by make and model any automobile she saw by age four. By age four she also could write her name and numbers and use numerical concepts, identify 48 different colors, and understand the sequence of hours in the day. She took dancing lessons at age four and was extremely well coordinated, advancing to an older class quite rapidly.

In school she achieved extremely high marks and could read seven grades above her third-grade level. Her achievement in other school subjects was three or more grades above level. She was a varsity athlete for four years in both high school and college and participated in every extracurricular activity available. She learned to play three musical instruments, two self-taught, and learned the rudiments of several others. She received several scholarships to college and was later offered scholarships to both law school and art school.

Beth's I.Q. has been measured from 130 to 145. She is both creative and intelligent and has attained high educational status and professional accomplishment as an adult. Her interest in music has continued as a hobby, and she also performs with a professional group.

These persons—Terri and Beth—could easily have been identified as being both intelligent and creative before they entered school purely on the basis of the kinds of things they did in comparison to other children of the same age. Beth's high academic achievement in comparison to Terri's is related to inner motivation, the level of personal rewards received, and the family structure in which she grew up. Beth's family allowed and encouraged independence and nonconformity in the home, but there was a strong emphasis on social acceptance and conformity in the community.

CHECKLIST OF BEHAVIORS TO MEASURE GIFTEDNESS AND TALENT

Gifted/talented persons tend to be above average in health, coordination, and the rate of both mental and physical development. Not only do they develop more quickly in mental and physical areas, but they also exhibit greater complexity and power in specific areas of development than do those of average abilities.

Use the checklist that follows to measure yourself, another, or a child for indications of gifted and talented behavior. For each item listed, check:

1. If the behavior is never seen (1 point)
2. If the behavior is seldom seen (2 points)
3. If the behavior is occasionally seen (3 points)
4. If the behavior is seen fairly often (4 points)
5. If the behavior occurs most of the time (5 points)

I. Intellectual Intelligence

	(1) never	(2) seldom	(3) occasionally	(4) often	(5) almost always
(AS A CHILD)					
1. Chooses older playmates	___	___	✓	___	___
2. Gets along well with adults	___	___	✓	___	✓

	(1) never	(2) seldom	(3) occasionally	(4) often	(5) almost always
3. Prefers adult company to that of peers			✓		
4. Enjoys reading biography/ autobiography, reference books	✓	✓			

(ALL AGES)

	(1) never	(2) seldom	(3) occasionally	(4) often	(5) almost always
5. Curious and inquisitive			✓		✓
6. Has large vocabulary				✓	✓
7. Uses language fluently and richly			✓		✓
8. Enjoys reading			✓		✓
9. Has abundance of ideas				✓	
10. Has excellent memory			✓		✓
11. Has large bank of information				✓	✓
12. Has sharp sense of time			✓	✓	
13. Learns quickly and easily			✓		✓
14. Notes and uses detail			✓		✓
15. Comes up with answers quickly, easily		✓			✓

	(1) never	(2) seldom	(3) occasionally	(4) often	(5) almost always
16. Answers are considered, appropriate				✓	
17. Quickly understands cause-effect				✓	
18. Likes school—likes learning			✓		
19. Understands ideas quickly, easily		✓			
20. Can apply learning from one situation to another			✓		
21. Finishes tasks started		✓			
22. Is well organized		✓			
23. Has mental and physical energy				✓	
24. Is industrious			✓		
25. Has strong self-motivation			✓		
26. Can work independently			✓		
27. Is highly competitive			✓		
28. Has high personal standards		✓			

	(1) never	(2) seldom	(3) occasionally	(4) often	(5) almost always
29. Has strong sense of justice	___	___	___	✓	✓
30. Enjoys puzzles and mental games	___	___	___	✓	✓
31. Has common sense	___	___	___		✓
32. Has (had) high school marks (over 90)	___	___	___	✓	✓

	below 90	90-109	110-119	120-129	130+
33. I.Q.	___	✓	___	✓	___

(If I.Q. is 150+, score 6 points) _____

Scores: 33-52 (low) _____

53-78 (average) _____

79-105 (bright) _____

106-132 (superior) _✓_

133-165 (gifted) _✓_

166 and over (super-gifted) _____

(See additional behaviors at end of checklist) _____

II. Creativity

	(1) never	(2) seldom	(3) occasionally	(4) often	(5) almost always
1. Is flexible in thought and action	___	___	___	✓	___

	(1) never	(2) seldom	(3) occasionally	(4) often	(5) almost always
2. Can live and deal with uncertainty				✓	
3. Has profusion of ideas, solutions, etc.					✓
4. Ideas, solutions, etc. are unique and original				✓	
5. Is personally independent			✓		
6. Is uninhibited				✓	
7. Is adventurous				✓	
8. Is inventive			✓		
9. Fantasizes, daydreams					✓
10. Has rich imagination					✓
11. Uses a lot of elaboration and detail				✓	
12. Is not afraid to be different					✓
13. Takes risks					✓
14. Questions the status quo					✓
15. Offers constructive criticism					✓

	(1) never	(2) seldom	(3) occasionally	(4) often	(5) almost always
16. Offers constructive alternatives	____	____	____	____	____
17. Concerned with changing, innovating, improving	____	____	____	____	____
18. Is sensitive to beauty	____	____	____	____	____
19. Is sensitive to other people	____	____	____	____	____
20. Is very self aware	____	____	____	____	____
21. Is highly self-honest	____	____	____	____	____
22. Has keen (and perhaps unusual) sense of humor	____	____	____	____	____
23. May be outgoing or may be withdrawn, but has strong self-assurance in personal projects	____	____	____	____	____
24. Emotionally stable	____	____	____	____	____
	(1)	(2)	(3)	(4)	(5)

	never	seldom	occasionally	often	almost always
(BUT AT TIMES MAY BE)					
25. excitable	___	___	___	✓	✓
26. moody	___	___	___	✓	___
27. irritable (especially if interrupted during per- sonal activities)	___	___	___	✓	✓
28. Dislikes routine and repetition	___	___	___	___	✓
29. Likes to work toward goal, product	___	___	___	✓	✓
30. Can see the "whole" quickly	___	___	✓	___	✓
31. Strong sense of proportion and balance (visually, men- tally, physically)	___	___	✓	✓	___
32. When given a choice, cho- oses activities requiring cre- ative endeavor	___	___	___	✓	___

Scores: 32-47 (creatively inhibited)_____

48-75 (average creativity) _____

76-91 (above average creativity) _____

92-128 (superior creativity) _____

129-160 (creatively talented) 😊 _____

III. Social/Personal/Leadership

	(1) never	(2) seldom	(3) occasionally	(4) often	(5) almost always
1. Self-assertive			✓		
2. Bored by routine					✓
3. Becomes absorbed and involved					✓
4. Interested in controversial, adult, or abstract problems					✓
5. Likes to organize				✓	
6. Extremely concerned with morals, ethics				✓	
7. Sets high goals				✓	
8. Likes and takes responsibility					✓
9. Is popular, well-liked			✓		
10. Gets along well with others				✓	
11. Self-confident with all ages		✓			
12. Adaptable to new situations			✓		
13. Flexible—can change ways of getting goals without frustration			✓		

	(1) never	(2) seldom	(3) occasionally	(4) often	(5) almost always
14. Sociable—prefers to be with others	____	____	____	✓	____
15. Genuine interest in other people	____	____	____	✓	____
16. Is initiator of activities	____	____	____	✓	✓
17. A resource for others; is naturally turned to for guidance, direction	____	____	____	____	✓
18. Is open to differences in others	____	____	____	✓	✓
19. Participates in many social activities	____	____	____	✓	____
20. Is leader of the group	____	____	✓	✓	____
21. Speaks easily and fluently	____	____	____	____	✓

Scores: 21–33 (definite follower) _____

34–49 (average social skills; not destined to lead) _____

50–66 (above average social leadership skills; may lead at times) _____

67–83 (superior social leadership skills) _____

84–105 (socially gifted; leadership skills) _____

IV. Physical

	(1) never	(2) seldom	(3) occasionally	(4) often	(5) almost always
1. Shows excellent general health			✓		
2. Shows superior physical strength			✓		
3. Shows superior physical agility			✓		
4. Shows superior physical balance				✓	
5. Shows superior rhythm					✓
6. Is well coordinated				✓	
7. Is larger than average (child)					✓
8. Has high energy and pep				✓	
9. Moves with exceptional ease and flow			✓		
10. Participates in sports and physical games			✓		
11. Would rather participate than watch					✓

Scores: 11–17 (very low physical skills) _____

  18–25 (low-average physical skills) _____

  26–34 (strong-average physical skills) _____

  35–43 (superior physical skills) _____

  44–55 (gifted in psychomotor skills) _____

Those persons who are clearly gifted and talented often are outstanding in more than one of the above areas. Total scores for overall giftedness and talent are:

  97–151 (low range of abilities) _____

  152–229 (average abilities) _____

  230–299 (above-average abilities) _____

  300–388 (superior abilities) _____

  389–485 (gifted/talented) _____

  486 + (super-giftedness/talent) _____

In addition to the general behaviors listed, give an extra point for each of the following, as observed in children or in the childhood of adults.

Intellectual Intelligence

  1. Teaches self to read before formal instruction

  2. Collects things

  3. Organizes and maintains collection

  4. 1 point for each organized collection

  5. Maintains an interest or a hobby over a long period of time

  6. Uses scientific approach to thinking and problem solving (analytical, methodical)

Creativity (Visual Arts)

1. Likes and uses color with originality

2. Chooses art projects when given a choice

3. Good sense of space and design

4. Is sensitive to forms and shapes

5. Is sensitive to texture

6. Uses a variety of line, texture, color, shape in artistic creations

Creativity (Music)

1. Chooses music for activity when given choice

2. Can match pitch easily

3. Easily remembers a melody and can reproduce accurately

4. Plays toy instruments at an early age

5. Invents melodies

6. Invents instruments

7. Reads music easily

Physical (Dance)

1. Responds to music with coordinated movement of body

2. Can imitate gestures and movements with ease

SUMMARY

Preschool children who are gifted and talented tend to develop earlier than do their less-gifted peers in physical, mental, creative, and social skills, and their activities are beyond their age level not only in order of appearance but also in the complexity and power of the demonstrated behavior. Contrary to what was once believed, highly gifted/talented individuals are also generally superior in health, strength, emotional stability, and sociability than are less gifted persons. Whether or not these outstanding abilities are fully developed depends on parental attitudes and the types and number of learning opportunities that are available and prized, both in the home prior to entering school and during the school experience and in the school itself.

A child's intelligence will develop to its optimum potential only if the child is allowed to develop physically and emotionally and is encouraged to probe and question. A certain level of mental and emotional "tension" is productive to learning and achievement. The productive "tension" is significantly different from that in which anxiety is so high that mental activity and development are blocked and frozen.

In addition, all persons, regardless of intelligence or general abilities, do have talents and gifts in certain areas. These should be respected and nourished. The development of intelligence and creativity at all levels of performance requires structure in living which promotes the highest level of personal organization and the development of self-discipline. Highly intelligent and highly creative persons are able to provide more personal structure than the less gifted, but all need basic guidelines and rules for living.

Rigidity of rules will inhibit the growth of independence and exploration necessary for the development of intelligent, creative, physical, and social skills. On the other hand, over-permissiveness will promote equally nonproductive chaos. Common sense must rule as family guidelines are established, with reasonable allowances for variation in individual styles and requirements. However, all children—and even adults—have a basic need to know the limits of the rules and need consistency in application of the rules over a period of time.